Epworth Commentaries

General Editor
Ivor H. Jones

The Gospel of Matthew

Epworth Commentaries

Already published

The Book of Job
C.S. Rodd

Isaiah 1–39
David Stacey

The Books of Amos and Hosea
Harry Mowvley

The Gospel of John
Kenneth Grayston

The First Epistle to the Corinthians
Nigel Watson

The Second Epistle to the Corinthians
Nigel Watson

The Epistle to the Galatians
John Ziesler

The Epistle to the Philippians
Howard Marshall

The Epistle to the Colossians
Roy Yates

The Epistle to the Hebrews
Paul Ellingworth

The Johannine Epistles
William Loader

Revelation
Christopher Rowland

In preparation

I and II Thessalonians
Neil Richardson

The Epistle of James
Michael Townsend

The Gospel of
MATTHEW

Ivor H. Jones

EPWORTH PRESS

Copyright © Ivor H. Jones 1994

Extracts from the Revised English Bible are © 1989
by the Delegates of the Oxford University Press and the
Syndics of the Cambridge University Press and are used
by permission

ISBN 0 7162 0496 7

First Published 1994
by Epworth Press
1 Central Buildings Westminster
London SW1H 9NR

Typeset by Regent Typesetting, London
Printed and bound in Great Britain by
Biddles Ltd, Guildford and King's Lynn

CONTENTS

GENERAL INTRODUCTION

The *Epworth Preacher's Commentaries* that Greville P. Lewis edited so successfully in the 1950s and 1960s having now served their turn, the Epworth Press has commissioned a team of distinguished academics who are also preachers and teachers to create a new series of commentaries that will serve the 1990s and beyond. We have seized the opportunity offered by the publication in 1989 of the Revised English Bible to use this very readable and scholarly version as the basis of our commentaries, and we are grateful to the Oxford and Cambridge University Presses for the requisite licence and for granting our authors pre-publication access. They will nevertheless be free to cite and discuss other translations wherever they think that these will illuminate the original text.

Just as the books that make up the Bible differ in their provenance and purpose, so our authors will necessarily differ in the structure and bearing of their commentaries. But they will all strive to get as close as possible to the intention of the original writers, expounding their texts in the light of the place, time, circumstances, and culture that gave them birth, and showing why each work was received by Jews and Christians into their respective Canons of Holy Scripture. They will seek to make full use of the dramatic advance in biblical scholarship world-wide but at the same time to explain technical terms in the language of the common reader, and to suggest ways in which Scripture can help towards the living of a Christian life today. They will endeavour to produce commentaries that can be used with confidence in ecumenical, multiracial, and multifaith situations, and not by scholars only but by preachers, teachers, students, church members, and anyone who wants to improve his or her understanding of the Bible.

Ivor H. Jones

PREFACE

Over the last thirty years the contributions to the study of Matthew's gospel have been immense. Those who have immersed themselves in the massive literature cannot but be enlightened by it. Indeed, so many aspects of the gospel have been submitted to detailed monographs and articles that it might seem that there is nothing more to be said.

This commentary expresses a twin conviction that there is a great deal more to be said. First, it is born from the conviction that lurking behind the scholarly care are errors of method of profound significance. Vitally important mistakes have been made in the presentation of the statistics on vocabulary and style as scholars have attempted to identify Matthew's contribution to this gospel. This is of course not the place to argue that particular case. That belongs in the context of academic literature and the present author is preparing for publication *Matthew and the Matthean Parables*, a study which sets out a different starting point for the identification of Matthean method. But even a small commentary can have a complementary function to the detailed academic study. By looking carefully at the text even a small commentary can suggest how a different approach to the evangelist's method can open up a new view of the gospel as a whole.

Second, it is born from the conviction that the gospel encourages a responsible and creative attitude to discipleship. This conviction has grown out of a long process of reading and writing, of working with different groups, lay and ordained, from conferences and study groups, including seminars and devotional studies. These have added further strength to my picture of Matthew as encouraging and facilitating a responsible engagement with the good news of Jesus Christ. Matthew was not built on a single coherent theological base; it brings together traditions from different places and many of the gospel's insights emerge as a result of that process. It is this process which also makes it an evocative text, one which in my experience is particularly significant in contemporary multifaith and multiracial settings.

It is however impossible for me to express adequately my appreciation for all that I have gained from the work of others, from colleagues and friends, from participants in seminars and from those who have spent time discussing Matthew with me. Librarians too from many Universities have given me much valued assistance in tracing and making available secondary material. Nor can my indebtedness be represented in the brief bibliography which is appropriate to this small volume. I simply acknowledge how much I owe to others and hope that my own work on the text may add a little to their enjoyment and profit, in their reading of this, the longest and arguably the most widely used of the gospels.

Ivor H. Jones

All Saints' Day, 1993.

BIBLIOGRAPHY

Books

Bauer, D., *The Structure of Matthew's Gospel*, JSOT Press, Sheffield, 1988.

Betz, H., *Essays on the Sermon on the Mount*, Fortress Press, Philadelphia, 1985.

Brown R., & Meier, J.P., *Antioch and Rome*, Chapman, London, 1982.

Charlesworth, J.H., *The Old Testament Pseudepigrapha*, Darton, Longman and Todd, 1983–85.

Cracknell, K., *Protestant Evangelism or Catholic Evangelization*, Methodist Sacramental Fellowship, 1992.

Davies, W., *Matthew* (International Critical Commentary), T. & T. Clark, Edinburgh, 1988–1993.

Guelich, R., *The Sermon on the Mount*, Word Books: Texas, 1982.

Gundry, R., *Matthew*, Eerdmans: Michigan, 1982.

Hooker, M., *The Gospel according to Mark*, A. & C. Black: London, 1991.

Kimbrough, S., *A Song for the Poor*, United Methodist Church, USA, 1993, (cited as *SFP*).

Luz, U., *Matthew 1–7*, trans. W.C. Linss, T. & T. Clark, Edinburgh, 1990.

Markus J., and Soards, M., *Apocalyptic and the New Testament*, JSOT Press, Sheffield, 1989.

Matera, F., *Passion Narratives and Gospel Theologies*, Paulist Press, New York, 1986.

Orton, D., *The Understanding Scribe: Matthew and the Apocalyptic Ideal*, JSOT Press, Sheffield, 1989.

Rowland, C., *Mysticism, the Poor and the New Testament*, The Manson Lecture, 1992.

Stacey, D., *Prophetic Drama in the Old Testament*, Epworth, London, 1990.

Stanton, G., *A Gospel for a New People: Studies in Matthew*, T. & T. Clark, Edinburgh, 1992.

Articles

Brent, A., 'Pseudonymity and Charisma in the Ministry of the Church', *Augustinianum* (Quadrimestri Instituti Patristici), Rome 1987, pp. 347–76, now reprinted in *Cultural Episcopacy and Ecumenism: Representative Ministry in Church History from Ignatius of Antioch to the Reformation*, Brill, Leiden, 1992.

Green, H.B., 'Matthew, Clement and Luke: their Sequence and Relationship', *JTS* 40, 1989, pp. 1—25.

Meier, J.P., 'John the Baptist in Josephus: Philology and Exegesis', *JBL* 111, 1992, pp. 225–37.

Stegemann, H., 'Der Pešer Ps. 37', *RQ* 14, 1963, pp. 235–70.

Trevett, Christine, 'Approaching Matthew from the Second Century: the Under-used Ignatian Correspondence', *JSNT* 20, 1984, pp. 59–67.

ABBREVIATIONS

BCE	Before the Common Era (= BC)
CE	The Common Era (= AD)
HP	*Hymns and Psalms*, 1983
JB	Jerusalem Bible, 1966
JBL	*The Journal of Biblical Literature*
JSNT	*The Journal for the Study of the New Testament*
JTS	*The Journal of Theological Studies*
LXX	The Septuagint, the main Old Testament Greek Version
MT	The Massoretic text, the main Hebrew text of the Old Testament
REB	Revised English Bible, 1989
RevQ	*Révue de Qumran*
RSV	Revised Standard Version, 1952
SFP	*A Song for the Poor* (see Bibliography)
TEV	Good News Bible: The Bible in Today's English Version, 1979

INTRODUCTION

1 Matthew's gospel is a record of the life and teaching of Jesus of Nazareth, beginning with traditions concerning his birth and ending with traditions about his death, resurrection and final commission. It is a record particularly rich in sayings, parables and healing narratives, and its complex shape involves the interaction of teaching material and narratives (see 4.23; 9.35).

2 Matthew's gospel is popularly regarded as the most Jewish of gospels, written by a converted scribe (13.52) for a Jewish Christian congregation. The reasons for this are many: in Matthew Jesus says that he was sent to Israel (10.5f.); there are five great addresses, each ending with a formula (7.28; 11.1; 13.53; 19.1; 26.1), and they are said to be parallel to the five books of the law; there is an opening genealogy (1.1ff.); there are twelve 'formula quotations' from the Old Testament, together with the Old Testament themes of covenant, inheritance, blessing and curse; some parts have a rabbinic style parallel to that of Johanan ben Zakkai, the founder at Javneh (Jamnia) of first-century Judaism; and there exists a fourteenth-century Hebrew version of Matthew, which may well be considerably older; and there are rumours that it is the gospel's original form.

3 But there is a very strong scholarly tradition which maintains a quite different view, that Matthew's gospel was written by a Gentile Christian for Gentile Christians. The reasons are as follows: in Matthew Israel is rejected and it is the Gentiles who form the new people of God (8.11; 12.21; 21.43); the Great Commission concerns all nations (28.18–20); the Sermon on the Mount opens the fulfilment of God's will to every Christian (chs. 5–7); Greek wisdom terms are used; the ferocity of the attacks on Jewish leaders is almost unparalleled in the New Testament (see ch. 23 and § 13); and Matthew's gospel became one of the most used gospels in the ancient world.

4 Which of these two approaches is correct? Some scholars believe that the first approach accounts for the Gentile element in the gospel:

Matthew builds on the vocation of Israel to be a light to the Gentiles (Isaiah 42.6). But that does not explain the use of Greek wisdom terms which give the gospel a universal relevance. Those suggest that Matthew is not only building on the Jewish tradition but providing for a Gentile viewpoint also. So in fact both approaches are right: they are a measure of the gospel writer's achievement. They indicate that the creator of the gospel succeeded in producing a gospel which both Jewish and Gentile Christians could recognize as their gospel. It was a gospel which they could come to recognize not just as 'their gospel' but as a gospel available for all, of whatever race or background. The achievement was the product of a particular method. The creation of Matthew's gospel began as, first, a listening and learning process: the one who created the gospel listened to the various traditions about Jesus available in local Christian groups and memorized them. It continued, second, as a repeating and harmonizing process: the writer of the gospel repeated the traditions to various groups, so that the various groups became conversant with a story richer and more varied than their own. Different versions of the same stories and sayings were brought into line with each other (see 5.32 and 19.9), and a standardized language developed as formulae and stock phrases increased in number and frequency. In this way the groups were challenged to a greater understanding with each other and to share a common vision and sense of responsibility under God. This represents one of the most relevant features of the gospel for our contemporary world.

5 These two processes, listening and learning, repeating and harmonizing, can be identified in the language of Matthew's gospel. On the one hand there are hints of a single language which has been developed from various backgrounds: repeated phrases, the recurrent styles of story telling, key words carrying a variety of meanings; on the other there are hints of unreconciled traditions (a recent commentary has constantly to refer to what it calls 'inconcinnities'): variant expressions in doublets (sections which appear twice), contrasting styles and constructions within different traditions, containing different attitudes to mission, law, discipline, piety and eschatology.

6 The assumption is usually made that Matthew used sources, our gospel of Mark and a collection of sayings (often called 'Q'). That assumption is roughly correct, and is not inconsistent with the two

preceding paragraphs. It is correct in that those traditions were available to the writer; it is only roughly correct because there is no clear evidence that they were available to the writer in a word for word agreement with the sources as we know them now. Detailed study of the language of the gospel of Matthew makes it likely that the writer used the Marcan tradition in a developed form. So as scholars have compared our gospel of Matthew with those sources (Redaction Criticism) they have concentrated on a comparison of Matthew with written sources available to us and so have tended to pick up some parts of the processes of the gospel's development but not others. As scholars tried to see how the writer put all the material together (Composition Criticism) they did justice to the process of harmonization but not to the initial process of listening and learning. As scholars tried to work out the plot and sub-plots of the gospel (Narrative Criticism) they lost the episodic character of the whole story in a severely literary theory of how the gospel came to be.

7 Why then was the gospel of Matthew written down? The written form of the gospel resulted from the two processes which we have just described. Implied in them is an understanding between the writer and his audiences. These roles of writer and audience have been the subject of much research recently (Reader-Response Criticism). This method reads off from the gospel text an 'implied reader' as distinct from the actual readers. The 'implied reader' embodies all the predispositions of the text, and is therefore incorporated into the narrative. The actual readers by contrast stand outside the world which the narrative creates and can be moved by it, although they may recognize themselves in the negative or inadequate responses depicted in the text. Such reader-response criticism assumes that the interaction of text and reader produces a consistency of interpretation. Our view of how Matthew came to be written does not accept either a consistency of predispositions in the text or a consistency of interpretation by the actual readers. The roles of writer and audience are evident in the text of the gospel, but not in the way presented by reader-response criticism. The creator of the gospel reflected back the traditions which were known to the hearers, but reflected them back in an expanded way and eventually in a modified way. Such expansions and modifications caused tensions. Some hearers valued the traditions as they had first known them and resisted any changes to them. Some were satisfied with the exact repetition of smaller units and did not worry that further material had been added. Some

valued the additions and the modifications, especially as it became clear that these drew them closer to other local Christians. Some approved particularly the harmonization of the variants, the reconciling motifs, the emphasis on toleration and the broader vision; they valued the links with other Christian groups, and despite their differences over discipline, organization and piety they welcomed attempts at reconciliation with them. Because of these diverse reactions the process had to result in a written document; only in a written gospel could the reconciling motifs be evident and effective among all the local Christian groups, the conservative, radical and isolationist. Only in a written gospel could there be a statement of the entire tradition, with all its rough edges, with the opportunities for mutual understanding which had been built in to the full story. It was only in a written form that the story of Jesus could serve the development, reconciliation and missionary work of all the local communities which honoured the name of Jesus Christ.

8 There are a few hints of where and when the gospel of Matthew emerged. These provide an appropriate historical background for the processes and the relationships just described. Matthew 4.15ff., 19.1f. (see §§ 2E and 11A) suggest that the gospel viewed events from 'beyond Jordan'; we know from Galatians 2.11–14 that there were places 'beyond Jordan' where early in the history of the Christian church those of different backgrounds worked together and found difficulties in reconciling their approaches to mission, the law, discipline, piety and eschatology (compare with Galatians 2.11ff. these passage from Matthew: 9.10–13; 15.1–20); one of these places was Syrian Antioch, which was a metropolitan area inclusive of varied types of community, both social and religious. Jewish visitors from Javneh and Gentile missionaries from Asia Minor visited there; arch-conservatives and representatives of different (some might say heretical) theological persuasions held office there. Two of the problems traditionally raised against an Antiochene setting for Matthew's gospel are that Ignatius of Antioch (an early second-century bishop) uses only a limited amount of material reminiscent of Matthew's gospel,[1] and that Ignatius' understanding of his episcopal status is out of harmony with Matthew 18.18 (see § 9A). However the view which we have represented of how Matthew's gospel was formed assumes that there were different theological and

---

[1]See C. Trevett in *JSNT* 20, 1984, 59–67.

institutional views current in Antioch, and that the writing of the gospel may not have succeeded in reconciling all those who held differing positions. The date of Matthew is also relevant. It is likely to have been after Jerusalem fell to the Romans in 70 CE (see 20.7), especially if the gospel uses the Marcan tradition. A probable date for Mark was during or after the Great Jewish War (66–70 CE). The Fall of Jerusalem was a watershed for everyone, Jews and Gentiles alike. For Jews it meant that the promises relating to the temple and its sacrifices had to be looked at afresh; for Gentile Christians it raised issues about the continuity of God's work and the place of the Jews within it. All, Jewish and Gentile Christians alike, recalled the prophecies made by Jesus about the temple. So the development of Matthew's gospel spanned on the one hand the early period of Judaism's reformation under the leadership of Johanan ben Zakkai at Javneh and on the other a period of crisis for both Jewish and Gentile Christians as they attempted to come to terms with a radically new situation. The earliest known use of Matthew's gospel by one of the early church fathers may have been by Clement of Rome (*JTS* 40, 1989, 1–25, see I Clement 46.3) but there were early oral traditions which contributed eventually to the creation of Matthew's gospel, and the existence of those makes that method of dating unreliable. The Didache which has also been used in the dating of Matthew may also represent an oral period of the Matthean material.

9 What then was the contribution of Matthew's gospel to this time of crisis? It was to retell the story of Jesus in a way acceptable to many different groups. Acceptance of the Jewish Christian traditions meant a strong emphasis on the continuity of God's work in history (1.1), in the covenant, the law (5.18–20) and the promises, on the mercy and judgement of God (9.13; 3.12) and on the fulfilment of that work in Jesus of Nazareth (1.22; 2.15,17,23; 5.17). Acceptance of the Gentile Christian traditions meant a strong emphasis on the universality of God's judgement (12.43–3; 16.4; 23.36) and the power of God to create a new people (3.9; 8.11–12). Contained in these traditions were sayings and parables which implied personal and corporate responsibility before God. These stimulated a thoughtful response to discipleship through their openness to various interpretations and through their intriguing dialogues. It was with these materials that Matthew built a new kind of gospel which presented Jesus as the way for Jew and Gentile to discover and fulfil the will of God. It gave a new seriousness to the search; it underlined the immense tragedy

of human failure. Sometimes the hand of the author is evident, as in the parable of the Sheep and the Goats (25.31–45). Originally the material had served a different function, but it was refashioned into a summary vision of universal judgement in all its seriousness, when the standards which all recognize are given ultimate authority by Jesus, the Son of Man, the one who suffered and continues to suffer the injustices of humankind and who offers himself for our salvation and healing. While sometimes the hand of the author is evident, at other times it is hidden within the subtleties of expression and order which encourage the reader to decide what is meant and to take responsibility for the decision. The result then of the process of listening, memorizing, repeating and harmonizing was a distinctive theological emphasis which grew out of the association of those originally divergent traditions.

10 Our task is therefore to read the gospel and to engage with the text as the early hearers and readers did. It is not easy for us to know how Matthew's gospel was originally understood. The current situation in which the Matthean story of Christ was told gave it a specific challenge among a particular group of Christian communities, as it gave shape to cultic and institutional features of their life (Performance Criticism). But we can see how the traditions were used, providing a new opportunity for them to discover the seriousness of Christian discipleship. In this commentary we shall pause at key points to look at those traditions, to see how they were used, so that we recognize the freedom which was given to the original readers. That freedom helped them to find and respond to the will of God as shown in the Matthean story of Jesus Christ. The same freedom and responsibility is ours. This means that at times we shall distance ourselves from Matthew's assumptions and conclusions. That is part of the freedom which the text gives us. Above all, however, the presence of a text intended to help different groups to find a common purpose may encourage us, provided we are willing to use the freedom afforded by the text, to listen and discover new ways forward which as individuals and as communities we have not anticipated.

11 The outline of Matthew's gospel in the Contents suggests a way which someone memorizing the material might have used. The sections and subsections provide groupings of material which are useful for that purpose. The divisions and headings suggest to the memory new beginnings and new movements within the narrative.

COMMENTARY

§1 The Opening of the Gospel
1.1–2.23

A. The Genealogy
1.1–17

1.1 *The genealogy of Jesus Christ, son of David, son of Abraham.* The gospel begins as it will continue, allusively but powerfully. The varied translations of this verse illustrate the problem. In contrast to the REB some translations of v.1 add the word 'book'; the RSV begins: 'The book of the genealogy of Jesus Christ', emphasizing that what had been shared orally was now given a written form. Other translators prefer 'Table of pedigree'. For the word translated 'genealogy' in the REB can bear a host of possible meanings: genealogy, birth (as it does in 1.18), creation (with a reference to the book of Genesis), beginning, life or pedigree. The allusive language is characteristic of the gospel; and it has a purpose. The story which is to unfold concerns Jesus Christ, whom neither pedigree, nor title, nor national tradition can satisfactorily describe. He is the 'Christ', the anointed one (1.16f.), the expected Messiah (2.4), in the traditional messianic patterns of a healer and a teacher (20.30, 31; 23.10). But alongside the Davidic sonship are other claims: he is addressed as Lord by David in the Psalms (22.45); he is the suffering, judging Son of Man, the Son of the living God (16.16), the one who fulfils the divine covenant with Abraham, promising a blessing for many nations. So the allusive language widens the terms of reference for the telling of Jesus' story and enables people from many nations to sense the power of the good news and claim Jesus as Saviour and Lord. It is true that the framework of the genealogy and its position is Jewish (see Zephaniah 1.1); but any biography would be graced by a distinguished pedigree such as this (Quintilian, the Roman authority on literary etiquette, wrote: 'Before the life of a man there should come his fatherland, parents and ancestors'). So Matthew has a

1

different kind of opening from that of the other gospels. Mark's introduction mentions 'gospel'; Luke refers to his 'account'. Matthew calls his opening 'a book of the genealogy' linking the life of Jesus with the work of God through history.

1.2 *Abraham was the father of Isaac, Isaac of Jacob, Jacob of Judah and his brothers*. The line of the covenantal promise spreads out to include the twelve patriarchs ('Judah and his brothers'), and as the Old Testament offers an expanding and often surprising vision of God's creative work, so Matthew notes the expansion of that vision first in the promises to Patriarchs and then via the three pagan women and the wife of a pagan (Tamar, Rahab, Ruth and the wife of Uriah: 1.3, 5, 6). The Old Testament genealogies spare no blushes (I Chronicles 2.3–15, which takes the story from *Judah* to *David*) and the gospel incorporates the blemishes and disasters, the righteous and the unrighteous, in the line of Jesus Christ in whom God began a new and surprising work. New and surprising, indeed; but not without due preparation. That is the theme of the gospel and particularly of the opening two chapters. The living God has been at work for many generations, and the period from the patriarchs to David shows this (22.32). New beginnings are possible in the least likely of situations, and the past has still secrets to unfold which enable the new to happen.

1.6 *David was the father of Solomon (his mother had been the wife of Uriah)*. There is a muted reference to David's sin, as David ends one section and begins the next. The product of his sin, Solomon, becomes a new starting point. Unlike Luke's genealogy which traces the line from David via Nathan, the genealogy here gives the line of Jesus a Solomonic character; and following that Solomonic line Jesus is the healer *par excellence* (8.17), for Israel (15.24) and beyond (15.25–28). Unlike Luke's genealogy, too, the line continues here on a strictly royal route (compare I Chronicles 3.10–15 with Matthew 1.7–11) in violent contrast with the Jesus of later chapters, where Jesus is the suffering servant in whose humility the nations put their trust (12.18–21). The attempts to harmonize the Lucan and Matthean genealogies are unsatisfactory, as unsatisfactory as the attempts to soften the violent contrasts within Matthew. For harmonization destroys the nuances of the gospel, screening out its powerful allusiveness.

2

1.11 *Josiah was the father of Jeconiah and his brothers at the time of the deportation to Babylon.* Just as David ended one era and began another, so also Jeconiah (Jehoiachin – confused here with Jehoiachim and his brothers: II Kings 24.17) ends one section and begins the next. The period of exile in Babylon stands between the two, a witness to the reliability of God's promises in the Promised Land and in Gentile Babylon, and to the perils for all of disobeying God.

1.16 *Jacob* (was the father) *of Joseph, the husband of Mary, who gave birth to Jesus called Messiah.* The writer of the gospel is untroubled by the strange logic of this material: Jesus is Joseph's son (13.55) and a son of David, yet Joseph is not his father (1.18). It is the divine promise and its fulfilment that matters, what God has been doing through the generations and especially in the continuation and fulfilment of that work in Jesus Christ.

1.17 *There were thus fourteen generations.* The numerical perfection of the pattern (fourteen from Abraham to David, fourteen from David to the Exile, fourteen from the Exile to the Messiah) would have appealed to any Jewish reader and shows signs of Jewish symbolism. As it stands, the genealogy would have intrigued Gentile readers too, who also were acquainted with the restyling of ancient pedigrees to fit neat historical outlines. But central for both, Jew and Gentile, was the position occupied by Jesus Christ, spanning the end of the third era and the present. The Messiah gathers up this history of Israel with its times of greatness and of humiliation. He opens up in the present time a new hope for the outcasts, the aliens, the dispossessed and the misjudged. It is a powerful, allusive, encouraging story, used to widen the horizons of Matthew's own generation. It is a story for a multicultural, multifaith context (28.20) with hope, wisdom and responsibility as its key elements. They are part of a universal heritage and are based on the reliability of God's ways and works and on the new vistas unfolding in the story of Jesus Christ.

B. The Birth of the Messiah
1.18–25

1.18 *This is how the birth of Jesus Christ came about*. The section is full of surprises. V. 18, according to the REB translation, tells us to expect the story of the birth of the Messiah. But what happens is the story of Joseph and how Joseph is seen as coping with Mary's pregnancy. On the one hand there is Joseph, portrayed as sensing here the scandal of adultery (see 5.32; 19.9); for that was an appropriate category if there had been sexual relations between an engaged woman and someone other than her betrothed. On the other hand there is the real scenario, as it is revealed to the reader: Mary's is a supernatural conception (she was going to have a child through the Holy Spirit); and this designates not only the status of Jesus but, within Matthew 1, the fulfilment of the creative work of God's Spirit from the beginning of time.

1.19 *Being a man of principle, and at the same time wanting to save her from exposure, Joseph made up his mind to have the marriage contract quietly set aside.* The Joseph story begins: he has come to a clear judgement on the problem which confronts him: he must stand by his principles, but (the disjunctive 'but' is better than the REB 'and', since it underlines the importance of Joseph's compassion) he must also save Mary from cruel tongues (v.19). Then comes the dream (v. 20); it reveals to Joseph the true scenario: God's work of salvation has been planned from the beginning and is now being linked with the name of 'Jesus' (v. 21). The promise is given of the divine presence in Jesus: in fulfilment of the prophet's words, he is to be virgin-born, *Emmanuel* 'God with us' (v.23). The directness of the divine communication is staggering. Once again the book of Genesis is called to mind. This is the first of five references to 'dreams' such as those which guided Moses, Jacob, Joseph and others of the patriarchs. What Joseph receives is a divine assurance personally given and without any external mediation. As for the message contained in the dream, Joseph is addressed as 'Son of David' (v. 20); he himself is involved in the messianic story. He is offered comfort and encouragement, and part of this is the evidence of a 'formula quotation': *All this happened in order to fulfil what the Lord declared through the prophet: A virgin will conceive* . . . (vv. 22–23). The dream has the authority of its own immediacy (see 27.19); but there is a good deal more to it than that. The dream is consonant with the ways of God revealed in the Old Testament; it is part of the way in which the promise is made to come true. It is difficult to know just where the emphasis lies in this astonishing story. There is much to be said for emphasizing the content of the dream: The message of Emmanuel, God with us, associates the opening story with the concluding verse of the gospel and is confirmed in the promise made in 18.20: Christ promises his presence among the 'two or three who meet together in my name'. There is also much to be said for emphasizing v.24: *When he woke Joseph did as the angel of the Lord had directed him; he took Mary home to be his wife.* Matthew, like Paul, recognizes that vision and insight, revelation and privilege need to be perfected in actual obedience: Joseph *named the child Jesus* (v. 25).

MATTHEW'S USE OF THE OLD TESTAMENT

Recent research, particularly on the Dead Sea Scrolls (most of which are datable before 70 CE), shows that the text of the Old Testament was still fairly fluid at the time when Matthew was being shaped. It is often said that Matthew played fast and loose with the Old Testament on the grounds that Matthew's use of the Old Testament departs on some occasions from the translations which we have, that is from our English translations (RSV; TEV, REB) of the recognized Hebrew text (MT = Massoretic Text) or from the best known Greek versions (the forms of the LXX = the Septuagint). However, given the fluid character of the text around 70 CE, it is much more likely that Matthew used current alternative texts and translations which are not available to us. It is unlikely that the Old Testament was being misused. Some of these quotations belong to the traditions which the author of Matthew listened to and remembered. That can be said of Matthew's use of both the Marcan and the Q tradition. The Marcan tradition, for example, uses quotations which are close to the Greek translation of the Old Testament (the LXX) with a few exceptions, and on the whole Matthew repeats that tradition again with a few exceptions (19.5; 22.37; 26.31). The exceptions do not fall into a simple pattern.

Alongside these are two other groups of Matthean quotations: The first are introduced by a formula, the second are not. The first, the 'formula quotations', are twelve in number and they all relate to features of the life of Jesus, indicating the fulfilment of God's purpose in him: 1.23; 2.6; 2.15, 18, 23; 4.15–16; 8.17; 12.18–21; 13.14f.; 13.35; 21.5; 27.9f. With two exceptions these are all unlike the Greek translation (the LXX); the exceptions are 1.23 and 13.14f. 13.14f. is worth particular mention since it is a classic example of Matthean ambiguity: it could refer to Israel's loss of status (see Acts 28.26f., where that is the inference drawn from scripture and the text is identical with Matthew's) or, more appropriately in Matthew's context, to the possibility of forgiveness for all. The remainder of the formula quotations, without betraying the author's hand, use mixed texts which sometimes have what could be regarded as an unusual translation of a Hebrew original (2.6 has 'rulers', a possible reading of the Hebrew text). Characteristic of all of them is a portrayal of the vocation and life of Jesus, God's son and chosen deliverer. The second group approximate to the LXX and are mainly from the Sermon on the Mount or are quotations from Hosea 6.6 (9.13; 12.7), underlining the significant Matthean theme of 'mercy'. (Note that the REB translates Hosea 6.6 'I require *loyalty*, not sacrifice'.)

In recent discussions of the Old Testament in Matthew a great deal of attention has been given not only to the Old Testament quotations but particularly to Old Testament allusions; a good deal of weight has been placed on the kinds of text the allusions represent. But allusions are by definition brief and indirect quotations and it is unwise to draw precise conclusions from the text form of that area of material. Nevertheless the allusions contribute a mass of further evidence that Matthew's gospel is concerned with the fulfilment of God's purpose in the story of Jesus.

Among the allusions and formula quotations are those which link the Matthean Infancy Narratives with the Old Testament. Some of the allusions belong to material which Matthew inherited. How Matthew inherited them and the form of the inheritance is not clear (see the use of Jeremiah in 2.17f. and 27.9f.). Some scholars identify two traditions: a Jesus/Moses tradition and a Jesus/David tradition (2.1–2, 9b–11) which Matthew compiled using the formula quotations and a conclusion (2.22b–23, parallel to 4.12–16). There is much to be said for that theory, particularly because the original Old Testament story of Moses was expanded, as the evidence from the first century CE writers Josephus and Philo shows, with details similar to those in the Matthean Infancy Narratives. But a difficulty with the two tradition theory is that the division of the material into two traditions by content is not altogether corroborated by the division of the material according to the variety of vocabulary and syntax there. If, as we suggest, the compilation of the material was at an oral stage, it is not surprising that there should be such a lack of corroboration. The narrating of the Infancy Narratives would have taken place against different backgrounds. The vocabulary and syntax of Matthew 1.18–2.23 show Matthew was to a very significant degree dependent on those different approaches.

In conclusion, the important point to make is that the fulfilment of God's purpose in Jesus Christ is illuminated through the use of the Old Testament in many different ways, as study of the Genealogy and the Infancy Narratives has shown. This is repeated throughout Matthew: In Matthew 2 the focus is on Gentile homage to Jesus; in the Sermon on the Mount Old Testament Wisdom illuminates the will of God for all; in 8.17 and 12.17–21 the redemptive work of Jesus is associated with deliverance for Gentiles; by contrast others concentrate on Israel, or emphasize that Jesus is Son of David (21.9; see also 21.13 in contrast with Mark 12.17), or that Jesus is the suffering prophet (16.14). The gospel of Matthew uses the Old Testament in a way which cannot be forced into a single mould. It draws its inspiration from various traditions, and the strength of the resultant witness to God's work is one of its impressive features. In particular the formula quotations focus on who Jesus is, what he did and what he suffered, and find in his obedient suffering the secret of God's revelation.

C. *The Magi Arrive*
2.1–6

2.1 *Jesus was born in Bethlehem in Judaea during the reign of Herod.* Now the birth story gets under way, in the royal town linked historically with David and Ruth (1.5–6), and given a dating in Herod the

Great's lifetime (according to our calculations, before 4 BCE). But with the announcement of the birth barely given, there follows another story, the story of the Magi.

2.1f. *After his birth astrologers from the east arrived in Jerusalem.* (Magi transliterates the Greek work: astrologers is one possible translation; or magicians (see Acts 13.6,8); or 'those who studied the stars'). In the same way that the story of Joseph's dream in ch. 1 provided insights into the coming of the Messiah, so also does the story of the astrologers in ch. 2. Like Joseph they are already part of the messianic story; one of the Old Testament promises associated with the coming of the Messiah concerns an oracle 'from the mountains of the east' that 'a star will come forth out of Jacob; a comet will arise from Israel' (Numbers 24.17). The Magi come because they have seen a star; they have associated it with the promise of a coming ruler, and wish *to pay him homage*. The phrase 'to pay him homage' is one of only a few phrases in this story which can be claimed as characteristic of the creator of the whole gospel (see 2.8,11); the rest of the story, including the Old Testament quotation, is full of traditional phrases and constructions. So it is likely that this is a traditional retelling of a well known story. The name 'Magi' places the visitors in the same world of dreams and divine communications which we encountered in ch. 1. As in the case of Joseph's dream there is little hesitation expressed about that world, although once again scripture is used by way of an affirmation. Matthew narrates that the Magi came, that Herod and all Jerusalem were *perturbed* (v. 3), that Herod *called together the chief priests and scribes* in Jerusalem (v. 4), and when he asked for a judgement from them they confirmed the prophetic promise (v. 5):

2.6 *'Bethlehem in the land of Judah, you are by no means least among the rulers of Judah; for out of you shall come a ruler to be the shepherd of my people Israel.'* This verse concludes a section full of implications for multicultural and multiracial situations. Gentiles have been drawn to Jerusalem, as the book of Isaiah promised they would (Isaiah 66.18–21). But the fulfilment they seek is not in Jerusalem; it is in Bethlehem. Part of the fascination of Matthew's gospel is why the astrologers are given pride of place and why their search is affirmed through scripture. Far from being excluded, Gentiles are to have an honoured place in the new covenant. Jewish and Gentile Christians need to coexist in mutual honour as well as in mutual toleration and under a common judgement. Any why is their search affirmed on the basis of evidence from 'scribes'? Sometimes it is suggested that 'the scribes' appear here as a warning that Gentiles can see the light where the Jews in Jerusalem do not (as the 'people of Nineveh' are a warning in 12.41) or as a contrast between false leaders and the true leader of 2.6. The text does not imply that. Indeed we have already suggested that the evidence offered by the scribes actually affirms for Herod the astrologers' search. One of the great tragedies in the reading of Matthew's gospel has been the damage which has been done to Jewish-Christian relationships through its interpretation. There are enough problems to be faced in the reading of Matthew against the background of our own contemporary Jewish-Christian relationships without adding to their number unnecessarily. The scribes attest the Gentile search and they do so on the basis of a distinctive text or translation of Micah 5.2. Matthew's text of Micah 5.2 begins with the natural inference that since Bethlehem was the place of David's origin (I Samuel 16.1; John 7.42) and is to be the place where David's successor will be born, it can hardly be described as insignificant, for all its lowly reputation; and it continues with God's promise to David in II Samuel 5.2 that he will be Israel's shepherd. The promise in II Samuel is made specifically to Israel; the astrologers are seeking Israel's redeemer (see 1.21). So the coming of the Magi suggests that the relationship of Jew and Gentile should be of mutual honour: the One they seek is son of David, son of Abraham. (On this passage see the note: Matthew's Use of the Old Testament, pp. 5ff. above.)

D. *The Magi Worship the Christ*
2.7–12

2.7 Then Herod summoned the astrologers. . . . 'Go. . ., and when you have found him, bring me word, so that I may go myself and pay him homage.' Another of the links between the beginning of Matthew's gospel and its ending is the giving of homage to Jesus Christ. It is a characteristic theme of this, the first book in the New Testament, as it is of the final book, the book of Revelation. Sometimes the homage is hesitant, or at least for some lacking in confidence until Jesus inspires in them new confidence (14.32f.; 28.17–20). Sometimes it is insincere and treacherous, as with Herod here.

2.11 *They bowed low in homage to him; they opened their treasure chests.* For others, as in the case of the astrologers, homage to Christ spans the mystery between the joy (v. 10) and the humility (v. 11) of worship. The homage of gold, frankincense and myrrh, is open to many types of interpretation. Gold points to a royal birth, frankincense to divinity, and myrrh to the coming cross and passion. But the gifts are prophetic also in a different way. Rather than prophesying what is to happen to Christ, the gifts prophesy what Gentiles will contribute to Christian worship. They demonstrate that the moment that Israel had been expecting has arrived. God's time of fulfilment is with us. The contrast of true worship and false, between the astrologers and Herod, is part of Matthew's picture. A Psalm which looked forward to that fulfilment also stressed the redemption from exploitation and outrage which the coming King would bring. 'All kings will pay him homage, all nations serve him . . . he will redeem them from oppression and violence . . . May the king live long, may gifts of the gold of Sheba be given him!' (Psalm 72.11, 14f.). This Messiah is not a royal tyrant, in the mould of a Herod: 'He will not snap off a broken reed, nor snuff out a smouldering wick, until he leads justice on to victory. In him the nations shall put their hope' (Matthew 12.20f., quoting Isaiah 42.3f.). These contrasts are part of the good news, and Matthew's gospel gives them powerful expression: contrasts between the prestige of Jerusalem and the lowly status of Bethlehem, between astrologers and infant, between vicious tyrant and merciful Messiah. This part of the astrologers' story, like the earlier part, had been handed down to Matthew. A superb narration, it adds further dimensions to Matthew's presentation of the Messiah's birth. Within Matthew's gospel as a whole it is also a preparation for the story ahead. It is about homage, about the contrasts between joy and pain, humility and blessing, tyranny and release (see Leonardo da Vinci's 'Adoration of the Magi'). It is also about the practical and down-to-earth, so much a feature of Matthew's gospel. The kingdom of Heaven may appear to be about heaven, about spiritual piety and about the future; but it is also homage to Christ, offered as money, the cup of cold water, the help given to the prisoner, and here as gold, frankincense and myrrh, the gifts of the Gentiles offered to Christ before they return, because of a divine warning, *'by another route'* (v. 12; see Eliot's poem 'The Journey of the Magi').

E. *Escape from the Tyrant*
2.13–15

2.13   Joseph's obedience is now tested by a further dream. He is required to take Jesus and his mother to the safety of Egypt: *Get up, take the child and his mother and escape with them to Egypt.* They are to rehearse what many before and many since have experienced in escaping from tyranny or famine; and their story parallels what happens to refugees in many religions and cultures. The immediate safety of God's son is the paramount concern. Joseph is to take responsibility for him, as another Joseph did for a refugee caravan centuries before (Genesis 45.21–46.4), when God by a vision instructed Jacob to seek the security of Egypt, and as Moses did when instructed by God for his family's return to Egypt (Exodus 4.19). It is an epic story told in an epic style, that is in succinct, brief phrases, a style which we shall find elsewhere in Matthew.

2.14   *So Joseph got up, took mother and child by night, and sought refuge with them in Egypt.* The verse makes clear sense as a narrative (they come under cover of darkness to the place of refuge). It is less clear how early Christians would have heard it: would some have noted, as early church fathers have suggested, with pleasure or with displeasure, Jesus' residence in 'a godless place' like Egypt? Would they have made the symbolic link between darkness and tyranny, between Herod and Pharaoh, between Egypt and Galilee of the Gentiles, also a place of darkness (4.16)?

2.15   Matthew regards the residence as providential, whatever may have been the readers' reactions. It is to fulfil the prophet's word, *'Out of Egypt I have called my son:'* God has been preparing for this moment. Providence had been at work during Israel's history. That providence now becomes a feature of the life of God's son. Matthew tells the story as if the providential events of Israel's life, especially the departure to Egypt, were a preparation for another Exodus, the deliverance through Jesus. What God promised then is being fulfilled now. The quotation of Hosea 11.1, 'Out of Egypt I called my son', is however being used to recall yet another feature of this story of Palestinian refugees. Israel had to learn that God's providence was at work in slavery and in exile. That was true of the Babylonian Exile as will be poignantly recalled in the next section. Slavery in Egypt or in Babylon could only be ended by a God who could operate effectively and redemptively there. Whether the readers reacted positively or negatively to Jesus' residence in Egypt, they had to recognize God's sovereign power there. That demonstrated once again what ch. 1 had eloquently expressed, that through God's sovereign power the claim of Jesus was being extended and enlarged. Jesus' first visitors came from abroad. His first summons came while he was abroad. No refugee is outside divine concern and care (see *HP* 428), and this particular refugee affirmed that for once and all. For he is already a representative person: In Hosea the LXX has 'children' and not 'son'. There is already an indication of the oneness of Jesus with God's people. He represents them, as also he represents the Father (he is Immanuel). He represents the Father as the one who is called out of Egypt, the Messiah, the one who brings deliverance for all God's people.

F. *The Tyrant's Revenge*
2.16–18

2.16   . . . *Herod . . . gave orders for the massacre of all the boys aged two years or under . . .* This is surely one of the most poignant passages in Matthew's gospel. The story of the birth of the Messiah has begun. Visions and dreams have provided providential care and guidance. The visiting astrologers have reacted with joy to finding the Christ-child. Into the story is inserted the human cost of ruthless anger and tyranny. The slaughter of the Innocents in the narrative, as in contemporary life, seems to be the pointless venting of frustrated *rage*. Why does the slaughter of the Innocents stand here? Some suggest that the solution is to be found in one of the most famous chapters of the Old Testament, Jeremiah 31. It is the chapter that promises a new covenant written in the heart. It is a chapter of hope and promise. Even the reference to 'Rachel weeping for her children' (31.15) is immediately followed by the return of the lost children. Like the Three Pickled Boys of the St Nicholas epic the slaughter of the Innocents is soon to be reversed. But in Matthew it is not reversed: *they were no more*. The prophet is heard lamenting the deaths at Ramah (Ramah was in the Bethlehem area), and the massacre in all its horror remains unpunished and irreversible. Unpunished, that is, until the death which the angel foresaw (2.14) is fulfilled (v. 19). Tyranny is part of the Matthean story. It is part of the disorder from which the Messiah promises deliverance. It is part of the human cost of living under the power of those who know no mercy. It helps to explain why the Messiah must redeem from exploitation and outrage, and why the kingdom has a future reference. It shows why only one who 'will not break the crushed reed' can be a hope for the Gentiles. This Messiah is after all the Son of Man who will judge by standards of mercy (25.31) but who was himself subjected to an unjust trial (26.1f.). The slaughter of the Innocents is not just a background to the story of salvation. It is part of that story, to be faced in all its hideous folly and grief. The soldiers of Brueghel's narrative picture of the Innocents are real soldiers and the infants they transfix die daily. The fulfilment of which Matthew writes in v.17 would have been heard by many in this way. There is a pattern of destruction within God's world. Those who are responsible for it must hear Matthew's words of judgement. And no gospel sets out that judgement more clearly.

G. *Jesus of Nazareth*
2.19–23

2.19 *After Herod's death* . . . The section is parallel in structure both to 2.13–15 and 2.16–18; all three end with a formula quotation and indicate how extended passages would have been rehearsed and remembered. This section is particularly close in structure to 2.13–15. In both there is *an angel, a dream*, a direction (v. 20), and the direction is obeyed (v. 21). But in v.22 another dream intervenes, and with it a new direction:

2.22 *Directed by a dream, he withdrew to the region of Galilee*. It has been said that the first two chapters of Matthew concern who Jesus is and where he came from. That is a useful summary, although we have seen that there is rather more to the geographical references than that simple summary might suggest. What for example does the name Galilee suggest? A quiet, peaceful country area? We shall soon read Matthew's description of Galilee (§ 2E), or at least of a part of

Galilee. It is the place where the Gentiles live, where people lived in darkness and now have seen a great light. And there is *Nazareth* (v. 23). Part of our picture of Galilee is Jesus' home in Nazareth. We fill in the details with our imagination: we see Jesus in the carpenter's shop and reconstruct his life there. Matthew's interest in Nazareth was somewhat different, and at first sight less helpful. The move there was, Matthew suggests, in fulfilment of another prophecy: '*He shall be called a Nazarene*' (v. 23). But which prophecy? And is this yet another illustration of how providentially God has prepared the way for Jesus? The answer to those questions is by no means certain. No one particular Old Testament passage seems to fit Matthew's quotation exactly. It looks as if a good deal of Christian contemplation of the Old Testament had been taking place. This has resulted in meditations on the life of Jesus based on scripture, providing illuminating insights into Christ's mission and work. The three key insights are: '(He) shall be called holy' (Isaiah 4.3) – holiness and 'being a Nazarite' went together; and 'I have you called you in righteousness' (Isaiah 42.6) with a cross reference to 'a Nazarene restoring Israel' in Isaiah 49.6 (MT); and the meanness of Nazareth (John 1.46). Putting these together we can see how Matthew saw Jesus, the Nazarene. The Messiah is none other than the Servant of God, dedicated, led by the Holy Spirit, and called to bring restoration to Israel. Restoration for Israel and hope for the Gentiles were linked together; at least they were in Matthew's understanding. So v.23 summarizes a great deal of the first two chapters of Matthew. This is the story of Jesus, the Christ, son of David, son of Abraham, deliverer, redeemer, judge and representative of all humanity.

§2 The Proclamation Begins
3.1–4.25

A. John the Baptist: Repentance and Baptism
3.1–6

3.1 *In the course of time John the Baptist appeared*. . . The REB gives an appropriate indication of the general character of the time reference. Many Matthean sections use these general references; they are little more than introductory formulae. In this case it introduces material shared with Mark's gospel. Thus the second major division of the gospel begins with a reference to John the Baptist and his mission in the *Judaean wilderness*. The date, character and location of John are now known with some accuracy (see 11.7f. and §6A). But in Matthew's gospel at this point the information is inexact; there is a road which dips down from the Wilderness of Judaea to the el-Hajlah Ford across the Jordan, but Matthew's addition of 'Judaean' to Mark's 'wilderness' is probably a generalization (see §11A). It may be that 'desert' is symbolic rather than geographical: according to the Old Testament it was a place of refuge, of isolation, of demons, of Israel's pilgrimage and particularly of preparation, repentance and a future hope (see 3.3, quoting Isaiah 40.3 LXX in a shorter version than Mark 1.2f.; for the longer version see Matthew 11.10; Luke 7.27). More important than the geography and the symbolism is the relationship of John the Baptist to Jesus in Matthew. Their message is identical: '*Repent, for the kingdom of Heaven is upon you!*' (3.2 and 4.17). The kingdom which they both serve is one and the same. They have the same word of judgement, sometimes couched in similar wording (3.12; 13.49f.). They both present in their different ways the words of divine wisdom (11.19). They both draw large crowds. They each recognize that a similar fate lies ahead (11.12). They both have a body of disciples, committed to their way (11.1f.). There is a partnership between them which each recognizes and values: 'Among all who have ever been born,' says Jesus,' no one has been greater than John the Baptist' (11.11). Nevertheless John and Jesus are also very different. Jesus speaks of some of the differences in this way: 'For John came, neither eating nor drinking, and people say, "He is possessed"; the Son of Man came, eating and drinking, and they say, "Look at him! A glutton and a drinker, a friend of tax-collectors and sinners!"' (11.18f.) So like hairy Elijah (11.14; 17.12; II Kings 1.8 = IV Kings 1.8 LXX) John is described as wearing *a rough coat of camel's hair* (v.4); and many hearers of Matthew's story would certainly have assumed (incorrectly) from *locusts and wild honey* that his eating habits were ascetic, whereas roasted locust and the produce of wild bees were the best food to be found in a desert existence. Despite their closeness then, John is different in his style of life and movement. John is moreover only a forerunner (v.3): *a voice cries in the wilderness, 'Prepare the way of the Lord'* . . . Crucially important events in the life of Jesus will happen without John: he will be in prison, or have been decapitated; he will have no part in the major events which will flow from the Messiah's life and work (11.4–6,11). But to have been the herald of the Messiah, to have witnessed the messianic activity and recognized it, that is honour enough. John has, one could say, the right approach. He does not think of himself; he gives way; he speaks God's word whatever the cost, persevering to the bitter end on behalf of righteousness; and these are gospel attitudes. Not merely is he the forerunner, a voice crying aloud in the wilderness. He prepares the way of the Lord by the way he lives. In Matthew's view this way of doing right and proclaiming right makes John the ideal witness; he shows that it is obedience to the divine call that matters. As a witness he is astoundingly successful: *Everyone flocked to him* (v.5) and *they were baptized by him* (v.6) – boding no good for him under a wicked tyrant's regime and with potential enemies all around. Success brought mass repentance. The contrast between John's baptism in water and the coming of the Spirit and fire will follow later (3.11), but for the moment Matthew notes that those baptized were *confessing their sins* (v.6), signalling their commitment to a reformed piety through the purification of baptism. For John's baptism was nothing less than a once-for-all preparation of the whole nation; they *flocked* together for the imminent divine arrival, a coming which would mean both salvation and judgement.

(For a summary of the historical antecedents of John's Baptism see

Hooker, *Mark*, 39–43, although on Josephus, *Antiquities* 18.5.2, see
J.P. Meier in *JBL* 111, 1992, 225–237.)

B. *John the Baptist: Obedience and Judgement*
3.7–12

3.7   *When he saw many of the Pharisees and Sadducees coming for
baptism he said to them: ' Vipers' brood! Who warned you to escape
from the wrath that is to come?'* Matthew's version differs at this
point from Luke (Luke 3.7); in Matthew it is the Pharisees and
Sadducees who are dismissed as vipers; in Luke it is the crowd. In
both the tone is vituperative and ironic. Perhaps John disclaims
responsibility for their presence: Certainly it is not I who warned
you. Or perhaps John greets them with mock surprise: You are
unlikely people to have come within hearing of the news. Or, most
likely of all, particularly in the Matthean version of the story: it a
surprise to me that you should have seen the judgement coming.

Why is the tone ironic and vituperative? In the case of Luke's
gospel John the Baptist's words are directed at the ordinary
populace; the ordinary population would have been well satisfied
with a traditional piety which could provide hope of a restoration,
and John would be attacking their misplaced confidence. In the case
of Matthew the answer is more complicated, in two respects. First,
we cannot limit our answer to events in a single time and place; it
could refer to the time of Jesus or it could refer to the time of the
church. So it could refer to either, or both, of two stages in the history
of the Pharisees; it may refer to the time of Jesus when Shammai and
Hillel were the classic representatives of the various political affiliations within Pharisaic piety ; or it may refer to the time of the church,
particularly to the period after the fall of Jerusalem when the
different forms of Pharisaic piety exercised a tighter control over the
synagogues and through that control represented a threat to early
Christian groups. 3.7 could refer to either of those periods. Second,
we cannot be sure why in 3.7 the Sadducees were classed together
with the Pharisees. They appear together in Matthew only twice:
here, where there is no mention of Pharisees or Sadducees in the
parallel in Luke, and in 16.1–12, where there is mention only of the
Pharisees in the parallel passage in Mark. (In 22.34 the Pharisees take
up the questioning of Jesus once the Sadducees have been silenced.)
The question is therefore not only why they appear together in 3.7,
but why they appear together here in 3.7 and in ch. 16 where in both

places they differ from the parallels. In the time of John the Baptist there is a clear reason why they might be classed together. They had a belief in common that they possessed to a greater extent (in the case of the Sadducees) or lesser extent (in the case of the Pharisees) the means to hasten the fulfilment of traditional Jewish hopes. John the Baptist was amazed that they could ever appear to question those hopes, and he attacks that confidence. The traditional confidence in belonging to the Jewish nation has to be replaced by repentance and just behaviour (v.8) and a complete dependence on God's elective choice: *'God can make children for Abraham out of these stones'* (v.9). Although there is good reason why they should be classed together, the differences between Pharisees and Sadducees should not be underestimated. In the time of John the Baptist the Sadducees depended on their ownership of land and on the prestige which some of them, especially the high priests, enjoyed as a result of their temple power-base, a prestige which meant that they would be heard by the Roman governor; the Pharisaic influence, by contrast, depended on a fairly widespread acceptance of their oral regulations among the general populace as well as among the priestly families. But this situation existed only until the fall of Jerusalem. In 70 CE the balance between these two parties was fundamentally changed. With the fall of Jerusalem the Sadducees' power base was destroyed; at that point the Sadducees saw their social and political position undermined and the Pharisees were able to begin rebuilding their influence, using Javneh as a new centre for their work. In conclusion: There is good reason why Pharisees and Sadducees might have co-operated in the time of John the Baptist, despite their differences, there is no reason why they should be associated in the period after 70 CE. Why then do the two passages linking Pharisees and Sadducees appear as additions, 3.7 as an addition to the material shared by Matthew and Luke, and in ch.16 as additions to the material shared by Matthew and Mark. The answers usually given are that 3.7 shows how reliable the gospel of Matthew is historically; or that the author of the gospel added them as a later comment; those who claim that the author was a Jew maintain that a Jew would have added this as a note of realism, and only a Jew would have done so. But both of these solutions leave an important question unanswered: why, out of the thirty and more references in Matthew to the Jewish leaders, some of which are implausible for the time of Jesus, was the association of Pharisees and Sadducees found in these two places only. The best answer seems to be: the association represents a process of repetition and incomplete harmonization. The question whether the association is early or late does not affect the main issue; the main issue in the text at 3.7 is that of national identity and the claims of a nation upon God: *'We have Abraham for our father'*. To that claim John the Baptist responds with biting irony, and the most likely response for him to have made is: It is a surprise to me that you should see the judgement coming.

3.10 moves to the character of John's mission: *The axe lies ready at the roots of the trees.* There is a contrast between a baptism of *water, for repentance* (v.11), and the coming of *the one . . . mightier than I am who . . . will baptize you with the Holy Spirit and with fire.* He will separate the chaff from the wheat, and the chaff will be burnt. Matthew here is closely paralleled by Luke (Luke 3.16f.). Mark is similar (Mark 1.7f.), but lacks the reference to 'fire'. The Matthean and Lucan form presents two contrasts: the first is between water and spirit, between John's baptism with water and baptism with the Holy Spirit; and the second between wind (which separates the wheat and chaff as the *winnowing-shovel* flings them in the air) and fire (which burns up the *chaff*), emphasizing the judgement on those who do not change their ways (v.12). These two contrasts are not mutually exclusive: the coming of the Spirit at God's time of renewal and judgement involves cleansing and purification (Ezekiel 36.25–27). That was true of John the Baptist's baptism; it was true also of the early days in the life of the church. Of particular interest for Matthew's gospel is the association made in Acts between cleansing, baptism and Spirit. The words of Peter's vision 'It is not for you to call profane what God counts clean' are followed by 'John baptized with water, but you will be baptized with the Holy Spirit' and by the general recognition that the Gentiles now baptized in water have been granted by God 'life-giving repentance' (Acts 11.9–18). God has raised up new children for Abraham. In Matthew there are two further important issues concerning the Spirit and fire: first, it is not only John who speaks of wind and fire in Matthew's gospel; Jesus does so as well. According to Matthew Jesus and John taught in the same way. Both John and Jesus spoke of the winnowing-shovel being ready to prepare the chaff for the fire; and both understood repentance in terms of practical justice: *every tree that fails to produce good fruit is cut down and thrown on the fire* (3.10b;7.19). Like Ezekiel they both warn that once a tree has ceased to produce fruit nothing can be done with the wood except to burn it; and there is no protection for Israel if Israel does not produce the fruit of righteousness. Second, although both John and Jesus speak of wind and fire, there is of course a difference: in John the words refer to an imminent event; when Jesus speaks, he speaks as the Spirit-filled agent of God. The words have found their fulfilment. Furthermore those who become his disciples share the Son's privilege; they too are baptized in the power of the Spirit (28.18–20).

C. God's Son is Baptized
3.13–17

3.13   Jesus leaves Galilee and arrives at the Jordan; he persuades John to baptize him. There could be no better indication of Jesus' high regard for John than that. Despite John's disclaimer, '*It is I who need to be baptized by you*' (v.14 – a disclaimer out of keeping with 11.3), Jesus insists that John should baptize him. The reason which Jesus gives for this is unique to Matthew's gospel. In the REB it is translated (v.15): '*Let it be so for the present; it is right for us to do all that God requires.*' Literally the answer of Jesus is: 'Let it be for now; for thus it is fitting for us to fulfil all righteousness.' Righteousness means, as the REB indicates, human conduct consonant with the divine will, a rightness of life before God which is pleasing to him. It is a way of life which is a natural response to divine grace. So v.15, 'It is right for us to do all that God requires', is not just an acceptance by the Messiah of what God asks. It is a recognition of the divine work of grace in election and commissioning. Within that gracious work the submission of the Messiah to John's baptism has its proper place. God's new work is beginning, and in this Jesus' association with John has an essential role.

3.16   The baptism of Jesus is marked by the open heaven, the descent of the Spirit and the voice from heaven. *The heavens were opened* is phrased as if to draw together the gospel's dreams and visions, the Old Testament prophetic commissions and angelic appearances with the fresh relationship of heaven and earth signalized by Jesus. *He saw the Spirit of God* is ambiguous: To whom does 'he' refer? The gospel seems unaware of the question and offers no clear answer. What is important is that the gospel moves from the prophecy of John to what happens when Jesus is baptized by John. He has prophesied that Jesus will baptize with the Holy Spirit. Now the Spirit is seen descending on Jesus. The key to this passage is offered by 12.18–21, quoting Isaiah 42.1–4. From now on Jesus will confront humanity with divine authority; when he heals or warns or forgives or judges, it is God at work; he is the divine agent; he is the prophet *par excellence*; he is the Christ. He will act for humanity; he has shared in the preparation of the whole nation through the baptism of John as they anticipated the divine arrival; now the moment has arrived and in the descent of the Spirit he is disclosed as the representative one, humbling himself on behalf of the people of God for the sake of their restoration(1.21; 2.6) and on behalf of all peoples for the sake of justice.

3.17   The confirmation is given, as often in the Old Testament, by a voice from heaven: in this case the voice says *'This is my beloved Son, in whom I take delight.'* It is confirmation of a relationship which has one special feature among many: Jesus is in an obedient and loving relationship with the Father. He has already shown this in his conversation with John. He has recognized the gracious nature of what God is doing in his commission and has willingly submitted himself to whatever is necessary: 'It is right for us to do all that God requires.' The cost will be great, as 17.1–13 will stress when the voice is heard again; but his obedience will illustrate and expound the nature of the divine will, as it will also confirm the proclamation of the Old Testament prophets and of the Baptist. Jesus becomes its expositor and the means of its fulfilment; and because of his obedience and his humility, those who listen to him will discover the true nature of the divine will; they will find God's way revealed in him and the way of righteousness opened through him. Jesus' baptism by John promotes the hope of salvation for all.

D. God's Son is Tested
4.1–11

4.1   It is the Spirit which leads Jesus *into the wilderness*. There, *famished* from fasting (v.2), he meets the *tempter* (v.3). During the forty years of wanderings in the wilderness Israel was provoked into disobedience; provocation is the art of the tempter (see Job 1.6–12).

The leading of the Spirit suggests from the beginning of the narrative that such provocation will not succeed in this case. The first of the temptations (v.3) begins '*If you are the Son of God. . .*' Jesus is hungry and, like the people of God in the wilderness, he is tempted to assume that God has abandoned him and he must take matters into his own hands. What is at issue is his relationship to God. '*If you are the Son of God, tell these stones to become bread.*' In this way he could make provision for himself. But it would imply a loss of confidence in God, and the emergence of an anxiety which mistrusts God's care and providence. Jesus rejects anxiety, both here and in 6.34. Instead he refers to the divine will. The divine will is illustrated in scripture (Deuteronomy 8.3), and always seeks Israel's well-being: according to Jesus a filial relationship consists in seeking and doing God's will. Any other response to God is disastrous. Sonship consists in seeking and obeying God's word (v.4).

The second of the temptations (v.5) takes place on the *parapet* of the Jerusalem temple. It illuminates that same relationship: '*If you are the Son of God*' (v.6; see §14 J). But this time the testing is more subtle. Scripture is the way to discern the divine will. But scripture itself (Psalm 91.11f.) seems to offer a way of testing God's faithfulness: '*If you are the Son of God . . . throw yourself down; for scripture says, "He will put his angels in charge of you."*' In v.7 Jesus affirms scripture, but he rejects the devil's interpretation of it. The original term 'tempter' gives way here to the more familiar term 'devil'. Evil in Matthew's gospel takes many forms – evil spirits, false leaders, unjust rulers, and 'the enemy' of 13.39, the angelic opponent of God, 25.41; and here, as in 6.13, the tempter is the one permitted by God to test the chosen ones. But evil in Matthew should not be identified with the divinely created material world. The created world provides the imagery and context in which God's will can be discovered and fulfilled. So evil in Matthew is not a part of a cosmic dualism. It is part of a moral dualism in which all humanity, like Jesus, can exercise personal responsibility and choice. Correctly understood, scripture is the promise of God, not a way of testing God. To turn the promise into a test is to falsify the relationship; it is to turn filial trust into a kind of doubt; and this kind of doubt, or fearfulness, is destructive of obedience (25.25–27).

Associated with scripture as a means of sustaining an obedient relationship with God is fasting. Matthew alone in the synoptic temptation narratives uses the technical word for fasting in v.2, and Matthew alone distinguishes between a fasting which expresses the joy and confidence of the gospel and a form which is hypocritical and ostentatious (see 6.16f. and 17.21 in the REB margin).

4.8   The third of the temptations gathers up the issues of power and prestige – Herod has given evidence of what power can do – and this is a subject which will occupy the gospel writer later (see 20.20–23). What the devil offers (v.9) is a vision of uncontrolled and unlimited power, that is a power which denies the sovereignty of divine justice, mercy and love. The condition is therefore that, as Israel did in the wilderness, Jesus should forsake the worship of the true God (v.10). Jesus rejects that way: God alone is to be given homage; the values of his kingdom remain eternal. That again is the direction which scripture requires. Guided by scripture, Jesus chooses the way of the Son, refusing any but the kingdom's values, claiming nothing for himself and giving all the honour to God.

The temptations in Matthew therefore clarify the meaning of the baptism of Jesus. There Jesus committed himself to God's way. He would seek and do God's will. The temptations explain the significance of this. At the baptism itself there was a purpose to be fulfilled which they both, Jesus and John, recognized. The temptations go deeper. Seeking God's way is a relationship of trust in which there is no place for personal gratification and aggrandizement or for selfishness and greed; on the contrary it requires humility, mercy and justice. This has practical consequences for Christian living. It concerns the question of how the divine will is known. According to Matthew it is known by fearless, thoughtful seeking and doing of the divine will, following the way of the Spirit-led agent and representative of the new people of God. Jesus restores the ancient values of mercy and justice and realizes in himself this new and decisive fulfilment of divine sovereignty. Following him requires a fresh acceptance of responsibility, and that in turn involves a deep commitment to seeking God's way.

E. *The Messiah's Mission Unfolds*
4.12–17

4.12   John's imprisonment leads to Jesus' withdrawal north to Galilee, specifically to Capernaum on the sea of Galilee. Capernaum now becomes the centre of operations. It is where Andrew and Peter lived; and it becomes Jesus' own city, the place where many miracles are done. This is the start of Jesus' public ministry and it is to begin in Capernaum. Matthew pauses to reflect on the significance of this. In v.13 Capernaum is described as *'in the district of Zebulun and Naphtali'*. These two names belong to the tribes which were the first to go into exile. Ancient Christian tradition saw it as appropriate that it was where the Exile first began that news of the restoration of the kingdom should be given. Freedom begins where slavery first began. The quotation from Isaiah 9 picks up the two names and draws out their threefold importance . First, one of the great prophecies in Isaiah concerns the extent of the messianic kingdom: 'Wide will be the domain and boundless the peace bestowed on David's throne and on his kingdom, to establish and support it with justice and righteousness from now on, for evermore' (Isaiah 9.7). Second, the quotation in 4.16 highlights the new freedom offered by the restitution of God's kingdom; the dawn is driving away the darkness. Third, it gives a fresh emphasis to the names Zebulun and Naphtali. In the Old Testament book of Isaiah, ch.9 offers the hope of a new leader able to heal a broken people and names the different areas affected by the Assyrian deportation. Matthew is not interested in the list of different areas. What matters for Matthew is another aspect of Isaiah's prophecy. Isaiah had said 'Honour was bestowed on Galilee of the Nations' (Isaiah 9.1). It is, symbolically speaking, among and for the Gentiles that the Messiah has begun his work. The extent of the newly restored messianic kingdom is evident from the beginning. Such a reflection, based on the Old Testament scripture, suggests a twofold concern: first, that Gentile Christians should be affirmed, and second, that Jewish Christians should hear the affirmation.

Fulfilment is a rich word in Matthew's vocabulary. It is not so much a matter of predictions made long ago and now at last coming true. It is rather, as we saw in the discussion of Matthew's use of the Old Testament, that God's promises of hope and restoration given through the prophets have now at last been realized. God has been faithful to his promises. His providence has been continually at work. Faithful servants have assured God's people of this, and they have affirmed it through disaster and exile. Now in the ministry about to begin these promises have come to fruition. *From that day,* writes Matthew, Jesus began to proclaim the message (v.17). It is a decisive moment. Jesus has arrived in Galilee of the Nations: the ministry of the Messiah now begins to unfold in all its depth and breadth.

F. The First Disciples
4.18–25

Matthew now describes the calling of *Peter* and *Andrew*, and *James* and *John*. The story of the calling of the disciples, like the gospel itself, is one where the end is known before the story begins.

Matthew pauses to reflect on the momentous arrival of Jesus in Capernaum and meditated on that moment. The unfolding story of the Messiah is expounded in full knowledge of the Gentile mission. When the calling of the disciples is recorded it is in full knowledge of the history and fate of the disciples. Peter had been a leader of those who heard the story of Jesus. The consequences of his obedience in following Jesus were now evident. Those who listened knew that for Peter it had meant martyrdom. The stories of the disciples make strange reading against that background. They will give a curious impression of discipleship: Failure, distress, insight, courage, betrayal, denial, repentance, forgiveness, misunderstanding, and a little faith. The cost of discipleship will have been evident to the readers, as it is to us and especially evident the cost of immediate response to the call of Jesus, in leaving job and family at a moment's notice (vv.20,22). The challenge of the task, gathering in people as they gathered in the fish, gives weight to this and suggests that their work is to be parallel to that of Jesus himself.

The responsibility carried by these few will have been evident to the early hearers of the gospel. The humble beginnings of these leaders is in no way disguised. They were fisherfolk (v.18). Their status is clearly that of learners. They belong with prophets, martyrs, scribes, sages, not with rulers, officials, rabbis. And yet they have had to carry heavy responsibilities. They have had to understand, live by, interpret and apply the teaching of Jesus, and give guidance to Christian communities across the Palestinian, Syrian and Eastern Mediterranean regions. They have therefore had to carry responsibilities, sometimes without official status. In this respect their work carried the seal of their Servant Messiah. All this began for them with the act of obedience to Jesus Christ when he called them by the Sea of Galilee, and they could have had no inkling of the implications of their response.

The conclusion of ch. 4 is a summary (vv.23–25). The story has so far has been of promises, of prophets, of forerunners, of providence, of potential. Now all that John the Baptist proclaimed is happening.

25

John had promised that one would come after him who would baptize with the Holy Spirit and with fire. He had baptized Jesus so that between them God's will might be performed. Now the travelling around Galilee begins, and the teaching and proclaiming, the healings, the exorcisms, the crowds gathering from far and near to witness the coming of the Servant Messiah in the power of the Spirit; and with those events the restoration had begun.

§3 The Sermon on the Mount (Discourse 1)
5.1–7.29

A. The Introduction: (i) the Beatitudes
5.1–12

5.1 *When he saw the crowds.* The Sermon on the Mount begins with two groups. There are the disciples gathered around Jesus on the mountain (see Luke 6.20; and so far in Matthew only four disciples have been called by Jesus), and there are the crowds who are followers (4.25) and apparently (7.28) hear him out. But 'them' in 5.2 is left unspecified: *he began to address them* could mean either the disciples or all the crowd. The content of the Sermon leaves us similarly in some uncertainty about the intended audience. Sometimes the Sermon on the Mount has been regarded as for the few: it is so demanding that only the most rigorous of disciples could begin to match up to its demands. Sometimes it has been regarded as for all: the demands are so heavy that all must throw themselves on the divine mercy. The parallel in Luke's gospel, the Sermon on the Plain (Luke 6.20–7.1), poses a similar problem: that too begins with the disciples and crowds (6.17–20) and ends with a general reference to the people (7.1). We shall take the view that the Sermon in Matthew interlaces general evidence of divine generosity with specific forms of address.

The parallels are many between Matthew's Sermon on the Mount and Luke's Sermon on the Plain; in particular the two sermons have a common outline which begins with the Beatitudes and ends with the parable of The Two Houses. Some (as Augustine did) regard these two sermons as different versions given by Jesus of the same sermon. But even events that manifestly happened only once, such as the Last Supper, appear in variant traditions in the synoptic gospels. So variant traditions do not necessarily point to different times and occasions. As for the suggestion that they represent an original sermon of Jesus, the length of the common outline is against such a theory. The longest consecutive speech ascribed to Jesus in Mark's gospel is eleven verses; the outline common to the two Sermons is about thirty. The general view is that Matthew and Luke are offering variations of a common outline, that the common outline was known to them from a common source, and that the common source brought together earlier and quite separate traditions about Jesus' teaching. But in that case why was the common outline produced and why is the outline expanded in Matthew and Luke? Was the common outline produced to provide a convenient summary of Jesus' teaching? Summaries of disparate collections of material were as frequent in the ancient world as they are today. They were produced for teaching purposes, as are modern catechisms. Clearly Matthew had a great deal of material; indeed so much material had been gathered from different sources that Matthew has four further discourses, following a pattern similar to the Sermon on the Mount. But if the outline common to Matthew and Luke was a summary statement for teaching purposes, who expanded that outline and what was the purpose of its extended form?

Opinions differ on the extent to which Matthew was responsible for the expanded form of the Sermon on the Mount. Some think that Matthew 5–7 are an expansion parallel to the threefold Jewish outline favoured by Matthew's contemporaries: it provided an answer to Jewish opponents of Christianity, and its material is focused on law, cult and society. But in the text itself demarcation of three such sections is unclear. A simpler threefold pattern is probable for the Matthean Sermon: an opening (consisting of the Beatitudes, 5.3–12, and two headline statements: you are the salt to the world, 5.13; you are light for all the world, 5.14), the main material (built from already available units), and a conclusion (using the original outline's warning, parable and concluding formula). Such a pattern may well be pre-Matthean. If Matthew inherited the Sermon on the Mount in an already expanded form, it was probably devised for some such purpose as 28.18–20 suggests: in making disciples it is necessary to baptize and to teach what Jesus taught. Style, form and content make that theory a strong contender: that the original outline of the Sermon was expanded to accompany Christian initiation. But even if Matthew inherited the Sermon in an already expanded form, we shall find evidence that behind the creation of the Sermon on the Mount as we now have it there lies a process of listening and memorizing, repeating and harmonizing.

Turning to the Beatitudes, in Matthew their form and content are appropriate for the purpose described in 28.19f. Discipleship and baptism involve two forms of teaching: general promises and direct address. As far as form is concerned, the Matthean Beatitudes match that purpose. They are a mixture of third and second person: there are general statements in the third person (vv.3b,10) *'the kingdom of Heaven is theirs'*, and there is direct address in the second person (vv.11–12), *'Blessed are you . . . exult and be glad.'* The Matthean Beatitudes begin in the third person form: 'Blessed are the sorrowful; they shall find consolation'; these are confirmations of God's graciousness stated in a general form. (Contrast Luke's Beatitudes which have the direct form throughout: Blessed are you who now go hungry; you will be satisfied (Luke 6.21) – it is a particular group who will receive recompense for present discomfort.) As far as content is concerned, the Matthean Beatitudes stress God's graciousness; and they all stress particular qualities of life: the appropriate adjectives are – gentle, merciful, pure, peacemaking. Matthew hears the Beatitudes both as general confirmations of God's graciousness and as confirmation of the qualities of life which Jesus himself showed and which reveal that graciousness.

5.3   The key beatitude is here: *'Blessed are the poor in spirit; the kingdom of Heaven is theirs.'* 'Poor in spirit' is an unusual phrase, although it is paralleled in the Hebrew of the Dead Sea Scrolls (e.g. the War Scroll 14.7) where it has a positive sense: the poor in spirit assist the downfall of the wicked. The parallel in Luke has only the adjective 'poor' and may understand the adjective 'poor' in a socio-economic sense. As for Matthew the addition of 'in spirit' to 'poor' could hardly mean mean 'voluntary poverty' (i.e. those who choose to renounce wealth), particularly if the Beatitude is a general confirmation of God's grace; it can hardly mean 'those who possess little spirit', since the fainthearted, like the third servant in 25.26, are criticized as 'worthless' in the Matthean gospel (as they are also in the Jewish Wisdom tradition); it might mean 'those who acknowledge their poverty before God'. That of course requires further explanation: Probably the opening of the First Discourse is intended by the writer of the gospel as a parallel to the end of the Fifth and Last Discourse (25.31–45); the latter passage presents poverty before God from several different aspects (association with Christ and 'his little ones' in his continual suffering with the victimized, the unjustly treated and the poor; acting in accordance with the motives of care without thought of reward, responding in thoughtful and faithful obedience, sustained in this vulnerable and insecure style of life by the vision of God's justice, and open and humble before the universal character of that justice). In other words the acknowledgement of poverty before God in Matthew has roots in Matthew's understanding of God, Christ and the church.

To such the kingdom of Heaven belongs. Working back from our definition of 'the poor in spirit' we begin to see some of the implications of the Matthean phrase 'the kingdom of Heaven': it refers to the universal creating and sustaining power of divine grace and justice; it includes the decisive and costly demonstration of that reality in the spirit-driven agent, Jesus Christ; for those within and those outside the covenant it provides the counterpoint to pain (Matthew 5.4; Isaiah 61.1–3) and the fulfilment of aspirations and joy (Matthew 12.18–21); it involves the rooting out of evil, tyranny and selfishness. Some of the further aspects of 'the kingdom of Heaven' appear in the remaining beatitudes (5.5–12).

5.5   *'Blessed are the gentle.'* The Beatitudes are both confirmation of divine grace and a summons to a particular style of life. The word translated 'gentle' here is used by Jesus of himself: 'Take my yoke upon you, and learn from me, for I am gentle and humble-hearted; and you will find rest for your souls' (11.29). It is applied to Jesus on his entry into Jerusalem on a donkey: 'Here is your king, who comes to you in gentleness, riding on a donkey' (21.5). In one sense the translation 'gentle' is misleading. For behind the word stands the fundamental approach to God and to the world which we have just described. 'Gentle' in Matthew 5.5 has more to do with 'peace and the integrity of creation' than it has to do with softness and adaptability. It assumes that we are alive in God's world and discovering that fact is an essential basis for living. Most of the terms used in the Sermon on the Mount are of that kind. Jesus is saying: Those who learn to live in God's way in God's world (with the qualities of life, privileges and suffering which that implies) discover now or later a divine endorsement. The kingdom of Heaven is therefore a challenge to particular kinds of behaviour and attitude (see also 5.7, *Blessed are those who show mercy*), as it is also their ultimate justification (5.45). This gives *'they shall have the earth for their possession'* (5.5) a special significance; it takes up the promises of Deuteronomy about the possession of the Land by the Covenant people and points to the universal fulfilment of those promises in the context of world-wide justice (see 5.9, *Blessed are the peacemakers*).

5.8 *'Blessed are those whose hearts are pure; they shall see God.'* One of the central emphases of the Sermon on the Mount (and of Matthew's gospel as a whole) is the inner integrity from which right speech and action comes. The selfless loving attitudes of heart and mind alone provide the key to the behaviour of true disciples. But more than that: they provide a key to the ultimate mystery of the kingdom of Heaven, that presence of God in which the veil of ultimate reality is lifted and the rapture of divine love is known: *'they shall see God.'* The mystical aspects of Matthew's gospel are often overlooked. They are nevertheless vitally important for Matthew; they link practical discipleship, suffering and persecution (5.11f.: *Blessed are you, when you suffer insults . . . Exult and be glad*) with 'knowing God', and they do so by encouraging an imitation of Christ's own qualities of heart and mind, his gentleness, meekness, integrity and determination to see right prevail. They witness God's glory, and they enable that glory to be seen (see §9A, 16.13–28).

(ii) The Two Headlines: Salt and Light
   5.13–16

The Introduction has two summary headlines. They summarize the Beatitudes in striking pictures. Living in God's way in God's world enables God's glory to be seen. Salt is about the righteous preserving God's order; light is what Christ brought to Zebulun and Naphtali; light offers a connection with the picture of the town on a hill. For did not God promise that Jerusalem, set on a hill, would be a light to the nations? But that is not all. Salt and light are given a world significance: *You are salt to the world* (v.13); *you are light for all the world* (v.14a). The promise that Jerusalem would be a light to nations is fulfilled in the people ('you' plural) who are salt and light bringing glory to God in the sight of all the world. For the *town that stands on a hill cannot be hidden* (v.14b).

Salt is also associated with costly discipleship. It is effective when it cleanses and purifies. The pictures which are used here move and shift in the mind, helping us to see ourselves and the world in new ways. That is the way that Jesus used picture language and

31

Matthew's gospel reflects that method. Salt can of course lose its qualities. Here another theme is rehearsed which occurs frequently in Matthew. If the salt *is good for nothing*, it is *thrown away* (v.13). The Sermon on the Mount moves towards that conclusion. Hearing is not enough; action, thoughtful obedient action is required. Otherwise you are like tasteless salt.

The Introduction concludes with *praise to your Father in heaven* (v.16). Like the lamp (v.15), throwing light upon the whole interior of the house, God's children by the good they do enlighten the world, bringing God praise. That is the gospel's vital perspective – the praise of God to be shared with more and more (see the Great Commission 28.18–20; §15 D). This is an important element in Matthew's understanding of mission. It is the quality of discipleship which makes possible the universal witness to God's glory (see Cracknell, *Protestant Evangelism or Catholic Evangelization*).

B. *Jesus and the Law*
5.17–20

The second main section of the Sermon begins at v.17 with this crucial statement about the law: *Do not suppose that I have come to abolish the law and the prophets; I did not come to abolish, but to complete.* Jesus upheld the law as a way of knowing the Father's will. This can be seen in Matthew's use of Mark and Matthew's use of the Q material common to Matthew and Luke: Matthew accepted the Marcan material which upheld the Mosiac law, weakening some of the Marcan queries about the law (Matthew 15.10ff., contrast Mark 7.18f.; 19.1ff.; 22.32–37) and strengthening the claim of Jesus to interpret the law (in harmony with mercy, see Hosea 6.6, and sharing elements of authority with his disciples, see Matthew 9.8); Matthew also accepted the Q tradition, which stressed the call to righteousness by both John the Baptist and Jesus, with the affirmation of scripture implied in that righteousness, (see 4.1ff.), and linked 'the law and the prophets' (5.17; 7.12; 22.40). So according to Matthew Jesus upheld the law. Not only did he uphold the law, he fulfilled it. Fulfilment implies four elements: First, through an interpreting of the law (an intensifying of the law's requirements rather than abrogating its commands, and an overflowing of righteousness realized in and through his ministry, see 5.20); second, through an internalizing of the law (so that internal motivation matters as well as external obedience, for both community and for individuals; see 18.15–35); third, through a simplifying of the law (the law implies a radical commitment to God which human casuistry can evade, but which can be stated coherently in a unity of ceremonial and moral law, of commandment and summary, 22.36–40); and, fourth, through a universalizing of the law by means of extra-biblical moral terms and aphorisms. Jesus, according to Matthew, fulfilled the law in those four ways. The emphasis is on continuity: Jesus upheld and fulfilled the law.

5.18   The next phrase sounds uncompromising: The law which Jesus fulfils cannot change; every detail remains as secure as God's world: *so long as heaven and earth endure, not a letter, not a dot, will disappear from the law* . . . But although it sounds uncompromising there are three areas of Matthean compromise: first, Matthew makes a number of exceptions: like Philo and Josephus in their summaries of the law, Matthew fails to mention circumcision; parents may be denied their due; marriage may be renounced; and these omissions would not have been regarded by Jews as threatening the perpetuity of the law; second, the search for the Father's will was incomplete without what Jesus said and did; especially through his aphorisms and parables Jesus probed ways in which the law could be used, especially in matters relating to motivation, casuistry, ineffectiveness and hypocrisy; third, 5.18c adds that nothing in the law can change *until all that must happen has happened*. This additional phrase seems to say that the law is valid until the consummation of all things; when God's purposes are complete, change in the law will be possible. But the same phrase translated here by the REB *'until all that must happen has happened'* is translated differently by the REB in 24.34. 5.18c can in fact be translated 'until all that is promised has happened', or 'before all that it stands for is achieved' (REB margin); i.e. Jesus' work of fulfilment renders the law mutable. Is this then yet another Matthean example of imprecise language? Some of those who believed that Jesus upheld and fulfilled the law would be only too glad to think that with the coming of Jesus the law was no longer immutable. Gentile readers would certainly be of that opinion. Others, particularly strict Jewish Christians, who believed that Jesus upheld and fulfilled the law in every literal respect, would be glad to

33

think that the law was immutable to the end of the age. What linked the two different interpretations was the word 'fulfil' with its four-fold reference.

5.19 Here a further distinction is made: Matthew distinguishes *the least of the law's* demands, such as tithing (Matthew 23.23/Luke 11.42), from the weightier parts of the law, such as justice. The more important must not be crowded out by the lesser. Nevertheless there is a place for both; both are to be taught and both are to be performed. More righteousness, not less, is the aim. There has to be an overflowing of righteousness greater than that shown by the scribes and Pharisees, if the hearers are to enter the kingdom of Heaven (v.20). How that overflowing of righteousness is to be understood and realized, is clear from the Introduction to the Sermon (§ 3A).

C. *First Antithesis: Murder and Anger*
5.21–26

If it is correct that Matthew stresses continuity, in one sense the term 'antithesis' is misleading. To point out the mortal dangers in anger is an addition to the commandment *'Do not commit murder'*; it is not a correction of it. So some would even translate v.18 'AND I tell you' rather than *'But I tell you'*. In another sense however 'antithesis' is the right word: Matthew stresses fulfilment as well as continuity, and, as we have seen, fulfilment can act by way of correction as well as explanation. That applies to both aspects of the moral teaching of Jesus: the aspect based on human reflection and that based on life in God's world. First, human reflection. When Jesus talks about anger his hearers are well aware of what that means. They know its destructive power. He uses the language of everyday anger, and compares it with murder. His exaggeration is stimulating and renewing (I John 3.15). Anger and murder are set side by side: they both merit *being brought to justice* (vv.21f.), or even 'hell-fire'. This is not of course a full-scale treatment of anger. It has one focus only, anger erupting violently and senselessly. (This is obscured in the REB text; the original text of Matthew 5.22a may well have read: 'Anyone who is angry without reason', and the translation 'nurses anger' should probably be 'permits an outburst of anger'.) The epithets in v.22 express violence too (although not a crescendo of violence): 'addle-head', 'idiot'. Matthew is well aware of other aspects of the subject and in due course will introduce additional features of Jesus' teaching about anger, especially about the dangers of nursing anger. These will also indicate that some forms of anger have positive aspects, and will show how these other forms can be prevented from deteriorating into 'murder' (These discussions have many parallels in Jewish interpretation of the Old Testament and should not be regarded as unique: see 18.15–20 and §10 D.) For the moment the single focus is enough. Human reflection is one of the pillars for moral teaching, with exaggeration as a means of opening our eyes. The divine world is the other. This is a perspective which Jesus presents in new and compelling ways. It can be illustrated from the next example: the '*gift at the altar*' (vv.23f.). Property belonging to one party has been misappropriated by another. The law recommends a remedy: the offer of a sacrifice. Jesus makes explicit the need for the property to be returned as well. But that is not the end of the matter. First, the reconciliation should take place; but then there is still the sacrifice to be offered: '*come back and offer your gift.*' We live and work at complex levels, with each other and in God's world. Both are given a fresh perspective in the teaching of Jesus. Even ritual has its place, as a means of development and growth, individually and communally.

The two verses on settling legal matters out of court (vv.25f.) illustrate another aspect of the same approach. You can treat the verses on the level of advice from a Citizens Advice Bureau: You would be well advised to keep out of the courtroom, if you possible can. Alternatively you can treat the verses as about the divine courtroom: You will be judged at the end; so you will be well advised to settle your affairs with God before it comes to that. But Jesus does not seem to make that kind of distinction. The Citizens Advice Bureau level and the divine courtroom level are not so easily separable. The decisions made in the former have much to do with the latter. We are to make the decision in the former as those who are living with the latter. Of course the world as we know it and the world as God would have it are not identical. There is a distance between them and that distance is part of what Jesus Christ reveals: hence the proclamation of the kingdom of Heaven.

So the First Antithesis is exploratory, and the exploration brings together human relationships and divine judgement in fresh and illuminating ways. The everyday and the last day are not very far apart.

D. Second Antithesis: Adultery and Lust
5.27–32

The section begins by setting lust and adultery side by side. Just as anger and murder were given an unwelcome association in the First Antithesis, so are lust and adultery here (see Deuteronomy 5.18): *'they were told "Do not commit adultery." But what I tell you is this: If a man looks at a woman with a lustful eye, he has already committed adultery with her in his heart.'* Once again it is inner attitudes which take primary place. But what follows is the most blatant piece of exaggeration in the New Testament, and all the more memorable for that: *Cut off* what is causing offence! These are serious matters. Whether we are dealing with pornography or flirtations, the language of Jesus will not let us belittle the issue. He insists that these are issues comparable with life and death, and he wishes to shock us out of our complacency.

What is at issue? What Jesus is doing is to set alongside the Jewish regulations his own ruling. It was expected of teachers that they should do this. For example the regulations on divorce in Deuteronomy were imprecise: 'If a man has taken a woman in marriage, but she does not win his favour because he finds something offensive in her, and he writes her a certificate of divorce . . .' (Deuteronomy 24.1). So in the arguments over the rights and wrongs of a particular separation authoritative clarifications of the imprecise wording were essential; and who could give the clarifications except the teacher or the rabbi? In Matthew the formulation offered is: *'If a man divorces his wife for any cause other than unchastity he involves her in adultery; and whoever marries her commits adultery'* (v.32). Here as in Matthew 19.9 (although in 19.9 the Greek phrase used is different from 5.32) Jesus appears to be restricting the right of divorce to cases involving a serious sexual misdemeanour (see §11A). There is to be no quick divorce (and no right to invalidate a recent marriage) either on the grounds of passing preference or trivial excuse: 'my wife burnt the cakes.' So, according to Matthew 5.32, if a woman was divorced and if she married again, which would be likely at the time (and this is what Deuteronomy 24 envisages), an adulterous relationship would be the result. The only exception was to be a case of unchastity. Jesus was reasserting an ideal view of marriage and offering in addition greater security for the women involved. But Jesus is doing more than this. He is not simply adjusting an Old Testament rule by interpreting its terms. He appears to be introducing a much more fundamental adjustment, an adjustment of human relationships. The man too could be charged with adultery: *'and whoever marries her commits adultery.'* There is to be a mutuality in relationships. It is not just a matter of whether or not a woman had the right to initiate divorce in court. There is evidence that she may have had that particular right in Jewish as well as in Roman legal systems. What Jesus introduces into the discussion is mutual responsibility. Each is responsible to and for the other. They are to treat each other as responsible persons, the man the woman, and vice versa. This is part of what it means to live in God's world and to live with each other as if this is, in every respect, God's world.

E. Third Antithesis: Oaths and Plain Speech
5.33–37

The change of attitude which Jesus requires according to Matthew's gospel affects our use of language also. That is true of the Third Antithesis: oaths and vows may be acceptable by Old Testament standards; Jesus says they are unnecessary. The Old Testament has much to say about oaths and vows, about the circumstances in which they involve obligations and those in which they do not (Numbers 30), that there is an obligation to keep vows to God once they are made but no obligation to make them in the first place (Deuteronomy 23.21–23), and about the breaking of oaths and swearing dishonestly: In 5.33 *'Do not break your oath'* and *'Oaths sworn to the Lord must be kept'* are summaries which seem to cover dishonest swearing of any kind either between people or before God (see Psalm 50.14 and Leviticus 19.12). By contrast, according to 5.37 a straightforward *'Yes'* or *'No'* answer is all that is needed. The usefulness of this plain speech was evident in the early days of the church. A dependable *'Yes'* or *'No'* had much to commend it (James 5.12). But the statement of Jesus *'You are not to swear at all'* upholds the value of dependable, honest speech without giving a blanket prohibition on oaths. Oaths can add an element of responsibility to evidence given in litigations, as religious vows can express unconditional commitment within worship. But additions to oaths to increase their impressiveness are in the end self-defeating. They reduce the reliability of language as a means of communication; they may also involve the blasphemous and the irreverent.

Oaths sworn by the name of God, or Jerusalem, or some other holy thing are self-defeating in another sense as well. They rely on the holiness of that by which the oath is sworn; it provides a sense of reliability for a statement or piece of evidence. If however the evidence is unreliable, then an oath devalues what is holy; and that applies to the human being as much as to holy names and places (vv.34f.). After all, what is holy gains its holiness from association with God, and since God's holiness establishes freedom and responsibility as genuine possibilities, the devaluing of freedom and responsibility is a serious betrayal of that holiness. This explains what follows in v.37. *'Anything beyond that comes from the evil one.'* (On the nature of evil in Matthew's gospel see §2D.) The Matthean proclamation of the kingdom of Heaven provides an alternative scenario to a dualism of God versus evil: according to Matthew, the world belongs to God and always will, and evil has to be understood within that context. Evil is the futile attempt to deny God and all the values which God sustains. From that point of view dishonesty and mockery of what is holy do matter; and even if the final phrase of v.37 has a touch of rhetoric about it, sharing the startling exaggeration to be found in all the antitheses, nevertheless the motivation for plain and honest speech begins in commitment to God's holiness, and to the justice, mercy and truth which flow from it.

F. Fourth Antithesis: Paying Back and Giving
5.38–42

Three times the law presents the principle of retaliation: *'An eye for an eye, a tooth for a tooth'*: Exodus 21.24; Leviticus 24.20; Deuteronomy 19.21. It is a principle which guarantees justice for the injured party while protecting the injurer from unlimited revenge. In the REB the response of Jesus to this principle is given as '*Do not resist those who wrong you*' (v.39). This obscures two features of the original text: the verb could refer to legal proceedings and the object to be resisted is described as 'evil', i.e. 'Do not confront an evil person in court.' Jesus is saying 'Do without your rights, even for the sake of restraining evil.' He gives three examples. Do without your right for redress, when someone insults you (v.39). Do without your legal right to retain one piece of clothing to cover you (v.40; see Exodus 22.25f.; Deuteronomy 24.12f.). Do without your right to limit the demands which authority places on you (v.41). The literal fulfilment of what Jesus requires has always proved problematic. The early church wrestled with this in many different contexts, sometimes accepting it as a ban on all resistance (as the REB implies). In Corinth the issue arose of taking a Christian to court for a secular hearing (I Corinthians 6). Paul's advice included a veiled reference to Jesus' teaching, suggesting that his readers, by standing on their rights, had already fallen short of the Christian ideal. The focus however should be not on its literal fulfilment but on the central issue: how the circle of retaliation can be broken, as is illustrated in the Passion Narrative.

5.42   probably moves from the area of legal obligation to that of moral obligation, although some, mistakenly perhaps, regard *to borrow* as implying an inability to pay interest on a loan. As a piece of moral advice '*Give to anyone who asks*' is unwise (Proverbs 11.15). In many circumstances today most people would hesitate to comply with it, although certainly Old Testament sources regarded the giving of loans as a privilege (Deuteronomy 15.6–8) So what kind of teaching is this? The phrase '*do not turn your back on anyone*' contains a hint of what is intended: both in Matthew and in Luke 'lending' is about treating people as people and not as elements in a social landscape or as opportunities for social or financial advance.

G. Fifth Antithesis: Enemies and Neighbours
5.43–48

5.43   gives a form of Leviticus 19.18 which has a parallel only in the Dead Sea Scrolls: '*Love your neighbour and hate your enemy*'; the second phrase is read as an inference from the first. Behind the response of Jesus *'Love your enemies and pray for your persecutors'* is a much more radical issue. It is an invitation to a style of life which will be capable of surprising the world. It will not fit in with normal expectations and it is an invitation from one who himself showed the power of the unexpected response. But this section takes us even deeper. For a second pillar of Jesus' teaching is, as we have seen, discovering how to live in God's world. The surprising feature of that world is that it does not work as we might have expected it to. It is a surprising place to live in. We anticipate that, because God is just and right and good, justice, right and goodness will be reflected in the nature of the cosmos (v.45). Instead we discover that there is no such distinction. When it comes to rain and sun, the rain falls equally *on the innocent and the wicked*; similarly the sun shines for those who are wicked as well as for those who are virtuous. The moral is clear. If God is like that, we should question how we usually respond to each other. We discover that God's world is a surprising place to inhabit! Of course the practice is as always harder than the theory. Vv.46f. reveal that in two respects. First, some negative pictures are presented: tax-gatherers and the heathen; the terms used indicate fear and hatred. Yet even these, as the 'lowest forms of moral humanity', set us a standard of mutual love and courtesy. What is asked for by Jesus goes way beyond that. But second, the negative pictures themselves, betraying fear and hatred, illustrate the problem. There is a great deal of discussion about the terms 'tax-gatherer' and 'heathen' in Matthew's gospel. They appear in a negative way again in 18.17. Some suggest that in 18.17 they reflect a Jewish Matthean attitude. Others, with good cause, see implied here in ch. 5 a multicultural setting where the teaching of Jesus has to be realized. For the two terms 'tax-gatherer' and 'heathen' may depict those within as well as those outside the Christian community (see 9.9; 21.23–27,31–32; 6.7), and if so would provide the crucial context of obedience for Jesus' teaching.

5.48   Again encouragement is offered: our *goodness*, like the goodness of our *heavenly Father*, should know *no bounds*. The REB translation captures part of the wealth of the original: Love unrestrained by social and racial barriers lies at the heart of the world and is therefore the calling of all who name God Father. The original text can however be translated: You must therefore be perfect, as your heavenly Father is perfect. Perfection implies here not only unrestrained goodness, but the perfection of heart and mind which has been the subject of the Sermon hitherto. See *SFP* 32:

> 'Ye shall be perfect' here below,
> he spoke it, and it must be so;
>   But first he said, 'Be poor;
> Hunger, and thirst, repent, and grieve,
> in humble, meek obedience love,
>   and labour, and endure.'

The Sermon concentrates on the singleness of intention and selflessness of attitude which directs and purifies action (19.21); perhaps, taking into consideration its introduction, we should add also, an openness to divine insight and wisdom. Perfection is a term which relates to the beginning of Christian living and its true culmination, linking initiation with ultimate union with God. This is the context in which disciples are made.

H. *True Piety*
6.1–18

The contrast between this section and the introductory headlines of the Sermon could not be greater. According to the headlines others are to see the readers' good works and glorify God; according to this part charitable giving, prayer and fasting belong to a secret relationship with God: *'and your Father who sees what is done in secret will reward you'* (6.4,6,18). The later addition 'will reward you openly' found in some manuscripts may be an attempt to reconcile the differences. This section differs from the Introduction, not only because of its emphasis on secrecy, but also in the spirituality which it presents: the Introduction emphasizes the kingdom of Heaven; it brings together corporate privileges and responsibilities, the universal sustaining grace and justice of God, commitment to God's mercy in the search for righteousness and obedience in attitude and action, and any thought of reward is qualified by the character of the kingdom. By contrast the section about charity, prayer and fasting seems more concerned with the security of religious activity and lacks the kingdom perspective, except in the Lord's Prayer, which appears from the otherwise perfect symmetry of the three subjects to be an

41

addition. The difference is partly due to the religious or cultic character of the three subjects and to the Jewish Christian character of their treatment (see Tobit 12.8–11, which specifies the same three subjects in a similar context, although the textual form translated in the REB omits 'fasting', and the context is public glorification of God). There are of course common interests between this section and the Antitheses, for example in the concern with inner attitudes; and in the context of Matthew's gospel there are ways in which 6.1ff. takes on other Matthean motifs (e.g. *'do not let your left hand know what your right hand is doing'* was originally an exaggerated attack on public display, and can remain so in 6.3, but in Matthew it can also become proverbial for the deeper motif of self-forgetfulness); however, 6.1–18 is in a different key from much of the Sermon, e.g. the treatment of forgiveness in 6.14f. lacks the emphasis on inner motives and attitudes which is crucial to the parallel in 18.35. This contrast between the Introduction and 6.1–18 is one illustration of the process of listening and learning, repeating and harmonizing which produced the gospel. Traditions drawn from different kinds of spirituality have been brought together; they are retained in part and harmonized in part. That helps to explain the detail of what we find here.

6.1   is a general statement: *'Be careful not to parade your religion before others'*: because it is a general statement the word translated 'right' elsewhere in the Sermon is here in the REB translated 'religion', indicating a summary of charity, prayer and fasting. Regarding charity (v.2), those who make a great show of their liberality are called 'hypocrites'. There is a hint in the word 'hypocrites' of a theatrical performance greeted by applause: *'they have their reward already'* (one of the meanings of the word translated 'hypocrite' is 'actor'); but hypocrisy goes deeper then pretence (see 23.23–32): it afflicts the heart and the will with a spiritual paralysis. Such a judgement on the religion of others is difficult to reconcile with 7.1; and one of the problems in Matthew's gospel is how to reconcile the harsh criticisms and references to hell-fire in some parts of the gospel with the commendations of toleration and forgiveness in others. Some parts of the church had disastrous experiences in some Jewish synagogues and this deeply influenced areas of the Matthean gospel tradition (10.17; 23.34; see also 12.14). The resultant tension is one of the gospel's problems but is also one of its great strengths.

On prayer (v.5) those who make a display of public prayer are also called 'hypocrites'. The criticism is extended by reference to private prayer: '*Go into a room by yourself, shut the door*' which makes both a practical point about how to pray (see 14.23) and offers a vivid contrast between outward parade and genuine prayer. The mocking of *heathen babbling* (v.7) is also part of the same criticism of outward show, rather than a critique of non-Christian worship or of liturgical repetition, although confidence in God's providence does affect how people pray: '*your Father knows what your needs are before you ask*' (see 6.32).

6.9–13   At this point Matthew introduces a supreme example of prayer, a model which can be used repeatedly. Although a prayer with a long tradition reaching back to Jesus, it is a nevertheless a prayer summarizing many of the concerns in the Sermon on the Mount. It begins with the nature of God as Father. '*Our Father in heaven*' (6.9), the Father of all, and that includes those who are evil as well as those who are good. The keeping of God's name as holy, '*may your name be hallowed*' has a negative and a positive aspect: the negative belongs with the warnings about oath-taking; the prayer implies our responsibility not to underestimate the holiness of God; the positive belongs with the recognition of the Holy Spirit's work in Jesus and in history. The prayer for the *kingdom* to *come* (6.10) is a key to Jesus' life and work. It is what is meant by living in this world as if it is God's. A vital thread throughout the whole Sermon is the obedient and thoughtful search for the will of God, in the pattern of Jesus himself (26.42): '*your will be done.*' '*On earth as in heaven*' draws together what is done on earth and what is done in heaven (16.19) as well as the need to change this world so that it becomes like heaven, truly to live in this world as if it were God's. Two elements of the prayer become of increasing importance in the remainder of the gospel: the practical needs of human existence ('*Give us today our daily bread*' 6.11), and our vulnerability to evil ('*save us from the evil one*'). Our need to forgive and our need to be forgiven are closely linked: '*Forgive us the wrong we have done, as we have forgiven those who have wronged us*' (6.14–15); the parable of the Unforgiving Servant (18.21–35) expands this. The limits to forgiveness are real as are the limits to receiving forgiveness. This is why forgiveness is not only what we must seek and offer in human relationships, but also what we must seek in prayer. Prayer, the activity of the Christian communities and forgiveness belong together with divine forgiveness as the key. Only because of God's forgiveness it is possible for us to see how we ourselves can be forgiven and how others can be forgiven. Only there are the real limits to forgiveness overcome and the world opened up to the divine mercy. One of the great puzzles within the gospel of Matthew is the penultimate phrase of the prayer: '*And do not put us to the test*' (6.13). If that is the correct translation (and we think it is, although recent versions of the Lord's Prayer have chosen 'time of testing' instead of 'test') it implies that God tests us, and that part of that test will be temptations such as Jesus endured under the Spirit's direction (4.1–11). Like Jesus in Gethsemane, we may desire and implore God that this should not happen (26.39). But that may not be right for us. What we are assured is that God will not let us be tested beyond our strength. For God provides us with the means to endure and delivers us from all that might lead us astray (see I Corinthians 10.13). The life and work of Jesus is a confirmation that God can do this; for this world belongs to God, and through God's providential care and Spirit, through baptism and through scripture, through the forgiveness available at the Lord's Supper and through the faithful community and its prayer, 'the evil one' will have no power to destroy us. Matthew recognizes that there is a place for fasting and returns to the subject on several occasions. In 9.15 it is clear that it will be continuing feature of the church's life. The recommendation here is for 'glad fasting'. The features of this are the inner attitude of repentance and humility before God, and the avoidance of maudlin impressions and showy expressions. 'Glad fasting' will link together joy at the forgiveness which is offered and inner homage to God.

I. *Singleness of Heart*
6.19–24

The unit on true piety, forged under Jewish Christian influence, is followed by another unit of a quite different character. Its three elements (vv.19–21, 22f. and 24) focus on money. The first stresses its transient character, the second the dangers of a greedy and jealous eye, and the third that it allows no rival. This apparently negative approach to money has two significant parallels; the first is in Luke (12.33f., 18.24–27, 16.13), and the second is in Ecclesiasticus (29.10–

31.15). In other words material common to Matthew and Luke has in Matthew been given a shape parallel to traditional wisdom. Traditional wisdom reflected on daily issues in the light of God-given reason and revelation: what does it mean to live in God's world and how should that affect our attitudes and behaviour? And it is used for reflection pithy and memorable sayings mounted in thought-provoking sequences such as the three elements represent here. This was a form of teaching often found in the sayings of Jesus, and its effectiveness in communicating with anyone and everyone is part of the rich secret of the wisdom tradition. Property and finance were favourite subjects of discussion, and the first three verses (vv.19–21) reflect on how vulnerable those are who rely on property: *'moth and rust destroy and thieves break in and steal'* (v.19). Better to use money and property for purposes which last: *'store up treasure in heaven'* (v.20); better to be committed to what lasts: *'For where your treasure is, there will your heart be also'* (v.21). The second element (vv.22f.) begins with a strange statement: *'The lamp of the body is the eye.'* According to this statement we can see because light travels from the eye: the eye is a lamp and its light is vital for sight. But in that case everything depends on the quality of that light. The words *sound* and *bad* move the discussion to moral qualities; and how disastrous if the light within is darkness: *how great a darkness that will be* (v.23). The clue to this puzzle is that a 'bad eye' (v.23) implies in the ancient world a greedy or jealous attitude. Such an attitude is disastrous for the whole person. The third element (v.24) sets up God and money ('mammon' in older translations) as exclusive rivals. This gives the impression that money is irredeemable. But in Matthew money can be destructive or creative, and both possibilities are set out there. It can be destructive of discipleship (19.23f.). It can also be creative: there are parables which use finance as a means of understanding the kingdom. The Parable of the Talents, for example, implies that money is among the gifts which we need to use well. We should not bury our talent in the earth. These two approaches, the one highly critical of money, and the other, highly positive, are by no means inconsistent. They are part of a realistic estimate of Christian responsibility. Money can enslave and money is transient. It would be very easy for those who deal in financial matters to lose track of whose world this is. There is therefore a case for choosing poverty. A long-standing tradition about Matthew's gospel is that it was used in monastic circles. There are hints of two levels of Christian responsibility, one for those who chose normal society and another for those who chose poverty. The latter had to leave everything behind. They could take no gold, silver or copper with them, nor a pack for the road. For these the radical warning against money had a literal significance. They had turned from the one master, and to serve the other wholeheartedly, with a single mind.

J. Avoiding Anxiety and Seeking Justice
6.25–34

Once again we have the argument from the natural world to the providence of God: '*Look at the birds in the sky; they do not sow and reap and store in barns, yet your heavenly Father feeds them*' (v.26). There is a natural providence which preserves the lives of the birds and allows the flowers to grow. Their beauty is given to them even though their lives are so short. Why then should human beings be anxious, supported by so gracious and generous a providence ? Some read this passage alongside the previous section on money. Those who have to leave everything behind and go on Christ's mission without food or money do not need to be anxious. The provision which God will make for them will be as ample as the provision he makes for all his creation. This fits well with v.33. '*Set your mind on God's kingdom and his justice before everything else, and all the rest will come to you as well.*' Those who commit themselves to a life of poverty are able to seek justice for others and in doing so will discover that they receive more than enough in return. The word 'justice' expresses the practical side of obedience to Christ. It means 'the doing of the divine will and purpose'. But Matthew did not restrict the 'doing of the divine will' to those who commit themselves to a life of poverty. What Matthew has to say has particular relevance to those with a calling to poverty. It also has relevance for everyone called by Christ to follow him. Determination to do the divine will is not the prerogative of the few. If Matthew recognized that there were missionaries living on the generosity of local people, he was also aware that the gospel would be heard by many whose daily responsibilities were of a different order. For them he advises: Do not lose sight of the kingdom; the kingdom involves doing the will and purpose of God. For all these the gospel with its parables will be an opportunity to see every part of their daily lives in terms of the kingdom. The decisions they make, the way they spend their money, their enjoyment of social relationships, their homes and their employment will be an arena for seeking justice. That is also the place where they can do God's will. The section concludes with a touch of irony: '*Each day has troubles enough of its own*' (v.34). As a proverb it normally has a pessimistic ring. Here it ends a section which says that there are no troubles for us to worry about. That gives it a humorous role and when read aloud would have been accompanied by a flicker of a smile.

K. Making Judgements
7.1–12

It is clear that living in God's world requires careful judgements. Discrimination is essential for those living in local Christian communities. There is the question, tackled later in Matthew's gospel, of what should be done about those giving false teaching or those rejecting common standards of Christian life together. Judgement in those cases is essential, whether or not it leads to the expulsion of a member who will not listen (Matthew's traditions are not unanimous on expulsions: 13.30; 18.15–17). Whatever v.1 means – '*Do not judge, and you will not be judged*' – it does not imply avoiding judgement altogether. It says simply but firmly: everyone is tempted to be judgemental; everyone is tempted from time to time to judge hypocritically; every community is capable of banding together to criticize and exclude. These are temptations to wrestle with, and we shall answer for our actions here and hereafter: '*whatever measure you deal out to others will be dealt out to you*'. The directness of what Jesus says makes it unforgettable: '*Why do you look at the speck of sawdust in your brother's eye, with never a thought for the plank in your own?*' The message could not be clearer; criticize others and you will quickly find yourself under scrutiny; criticize others and you will find your own credentials questioned.

7.6   however is different: '*Do not give dogs what is holy; do not throw your pearls to the pigs: they will only trample on them, and turn and tear you in pieces.*' The saying remains a puzzle, although it is clearly in place (as the parallelism between 6.19–34 and 7.1–11 indicates). Perhaps it functions as a puzzle; it intrigues and mystifies. Is it about the same issue as v.4: if you take someone to task, are you not liable to find your pearl of wisdom trampled underfoot and your good name torn to pieces ? If that is correct, v.6 gives the same conversation as vv.4–5 from a different perspective, as a humorous and sharp comment on the hurt feelings of people who find their 'helpful comments' thrown back in their faces – 'Don't give dogs what is holy! If you do, you have only yourself to blame.' Or is it about the hundred and one other circumstances in which a disciple of Christ has to offer comment? Is it about failing to make distinctions: 'What is holy and what is profane should not be mixed'? Is it about making too many distinctions, or making Christian community life a misery with intrusive inquisitiveness? Is it about leadership and its perils? Perhaps it is about restricting the time you spend with outsiders. But that again does not fit with the secularity of the Matthean outlook. Perhaps it is about keeping one form of teaching for the disciples and another for the crowd. But that is not what Matthew is doing here. Or is it a useful warning about what happens to Christians who teach in the local market-place? The puzzle goes on teasing us into fascinating reflections on how we make judgements. The reflections continue as we read on in 7.7. *'Ask, and you will receive; seek, and you will find; knock, and the door will be opened to you.'* For criticism narrows and defines; 7.7f. open the door on a limitless and universal promise: *'everyone who asks'*. V.9 brings 'asking' into a special focus, that of a father-son relationship, so that not only is the promise limitless, it is also useful and beneficial. Finally in v.11 the experience of generosity known in the father-son relationship is made the basis for a typically Jewish form of argument, 'how much more': *'If you, bad as you are, know how to give good things to your children, how much more will your heavenly Father give good things to those who ask him!'* The contrast between divine generosity and human judgement links the argument of the section with v.12, a positive version of the Golden Rule: *'Always treat others as you would like them to treat you.'* Just as the natural world provides an insight into the generosity of God, so also human relationships suggest that the Father of all will not be less generous than we are at our best. To treat others as you would like them to treat you – the positive version of the Golden Rule – is by no means only a secular guideline; as Paul also recognized, it is a useful focus for the whole Jewish tradition: 'that is the law and the prophets.' 7.1–12 shows that the Sermon is a sermon for all of whatever background or race, providing a basis for toleration (see 7.6 again) and building bridges between Jews and Gentiles, those for whom the law is central and those for whom the Jewish law is foreign.

L. The Two Ways
7.13–23

The conclusion to the Sermon registers the seriousness of becoming a disciple. There are two ways, and they lead in different directions, the one to *destruction* (v.13) and the other to *life* (v.14).It also registers its difficulty. The way to life is *narrow* (v.14); it is not easy to find. This may be a hard saying, but it is not without its parallels. There is the famous saying that 'it is easier for a camel to pass through the eye of a needle than for a rich man to enter the kingdom of God' (19.24). To live in this world as if in God's world is hard. And the Sermon on the Mount has illustrated some of the problems. To find the *narrow gate* and enter life through it means finding a new basis for living and for action, and human resistance to that is unremitting. In this search the teaching of Jesus gives us encouragement and challenge, giving a glimpse of the new hope and new possibilities in the kingdom. The world of divine providence and generosity points us in the same direction, as does our own experience. Among the difficulties are those who appear to be speaking God's message (*'Beware of false prophets'*, v.15) but are in fact as dangerous as wolves. The verse sounds as if a specific group of teachers is in mind. That impression is reinforced by the verses which follow. They can be judged by their actions (vv.17f.). The illustration is that of the fruitless trees being cut down and burnt (v.19). It is the same picture as in the teaching of John the Baptist. The false teachers can also be judged by their words (v.21). They call repeatedly on their Lord, claiming all manner of achievements (v.22). Perhaps they are the kind of Christians to be found in Corinth who identified miraculous activities as infallible signs of faith. Such teachers make the task of seeking and doing God's will all the harder. They divert attention and energies from finding the narrow gate. The way through the narrow gate is demanding and difficult, and lacks the public acclamation which the miraculous attracts. Never far away during the whole of the Sermon on the Mount, the motif of judgement here is central and explicit. There is the fire that burns the fruitless trees. There is the Lord who says *'I never knew you. Out of my sight; your deeds are evil!'* (v.23).

M. Concluding Parable: the Two Houses
7.24–29

The final parable of the Sermon on the Mount is that of the Two
Houses. In Matthew it is a contrast between the wise person and the
fool. The wise man *'had the sense to build his house on rock'* (v.24); the
other was *'foolish enough to build his house on sand'* (v.26). Wisdom
consists in hearing and doing; folly consists in hearing and not
doing. The parable therefore links closely with the previous verses. It
links closely also with the introduction of the Sermon. In a way it
summarizes the whole Sermon, which is about hearing and doing. In
particular it is important what the wise man hears. The introduction
to the parable places the emphasis on this. The wise person hears the
words of Jesus (v.24), and it is these words which provide the solid
foundation. They alone provide the solid foundation for those who
hear and act, and they are part of the fulfilment of God's purposes
through the work and ministry of Jesus. The two foundations remain
secure until the time of testing. The description in Matthew is of a
storm. *Rain, floods* and a driving *wind* (vv.25,27) batter the house,
testing the quality of the foundations. The rock holds firm; the sand
gives way, and disaster follows. Reflected in the narrative of the
parable is the nature of God's judgement. The false teachers appeal
to their Lord and receive the answer that he does not know them. It is
a powerful picture: apparent safety is suddenly and totally dis-
rupted. In Antioch the story would have woken memories of thun-
derstorms in the mountain above, sending destructive torrents on
the streets below. The words of judgement in Matthew are vivid and
powerful. The dangers they represent are very great. The difficulties
are many. Only those who hear and are obedient will find life. The
Sermon ends with a note of amazement from the hearers (v.28). It
marks the ending of the first of the five great discourses in Matthew.
It is not only the Sermon on the Mount that provides the foundation.
It is contained in four more great discourses. Matthew's task is to
enable that teaching to be heard. His task is to pass it on. It is the
hearers' responsibility to discover how those words make possible a
new kind of living, and to respond to the authority which they carry
(v.29; 28.18; 8.8f. and §4A).

§4 Miracles and Teaching
8.1–9.36

A. Acts of Healing
8.1–17

8.1 *When he came down from the mountain great crowds followed him.*
Matthew creates this narrative introduction (see 4.25) to move from
sayings material to narrative material, from the Sermon on the
Mount to the healing of the diseased man (8.1–4) and the healing of
the centurion's servant (8.5–13). There are various ways in which
this move from sayings to actions can be understood. It could be to
provide a set of messianic actions to corroborate the messianic words
(although not too much should be made of the 'mountain' symbolism – in the one place where end-time 'mountain' symbolism
ought to appear (25.31) it does not). The association of words and
acts could be a helpful approach to chs. 8 and 9 (see 4.23–25). But it is
also possible that the traditions which Matthew assembles (in
groupings which would aid the memory) are to be explored in other
directions or, at the very least, in other directions as well. Here are a
few of the elements. Matthew 8.1–4 raises problems of impurity from
virulent skin diseases (see the parallel with Elisha's healing of
Naaman in II Kings 5); Jesus also offers the crowds who follow him a
testimony concerning the healing (v.4, 'for a proof to the people'
RSV). REB narrows the meaning of this phrase unnecessarily: *'to
certify the cure'*, presumably because of the earlier phrase *'See that you
tell nobody'*; but see the Matthean editorial context in 8.1 of the 'great
crowds' and the comment on 8.27 below; it is a complex testimony
which seems by turns to infringe (*he touched him* v.3) and then to
uphold the ceremonial law (*make the offering laid down by Moses*, v.4;
see Leviticus 14), and so to require the man, restored by this healing
touch, to reveal what has happened through a cultic act of public
witness. 8.1–4 are partly an abbreviation of Mark, partly in agreement with Luke against Mark (see *'Sir'*, v.2 = Luke 5.12, translating

the Greek word *kyrie* absent from Mark 1.40; but see 7.22, 'Lord, Lord'; and why do both Matthew and Luke omit Mark 1.41 'moved with pity/or anger'?). These details help to cast doubt on the theory that Matthew has honed the story to make one specific point. The fact that Matthew has no apparent overall programme for dealing with Mark's secrecy motif (*'See you tell nobody'* v.4) is an additional warning against treating chs.8 and 9 as a tight theologically motivated piece of editing or even a formal literary interweaving of theological motifs or plots. The healing of the centurion's servant (8.5–13) *'as Jesus entered Capernaum'* adds further elements; the story concerns particularly the authority of Jesus (although prophetic authority is by no means absent from 8.1–4; compare 8.2 'bowed before him' with Obadiah before Elijah in I Kings 18.7). It emphasizes his authority by the way he heals. The Roman centurion uses his own experience of receiving and giving orders to express his profound faith in what Jesus can do (*'I am myself under orders, with soldiers under me'* v.9): a word from Jesus is all that is necessary : *'You need only say the word and my servant will be cured'* (v.8; see also 8.16). And the centurion's confidence is fully justified. Jesus in astonishment commends his faith to the accompanying crowd, gives the word, and the servant is healed just as the centurion believed he would be (' *"As you have believed, so let it be." At that very moment the boy recovered'*, v.13, a significantly Matthean verse). But Jesus' commendation of the centurion's faith (and in part Matthew differs from the Lucan and Johannine versions: Luke 7.1–10 and John 4.46–54) exposes a different framework for the story: a Gentile has demonstrated faith and this contrasts sharply with what Jesus had experienced in Israel: *'nowhere in Israel have I found such faith'* (v.10). The contrast leads Jesus to offer a prophetic vision: People will come from all over the world to share with *Abraham, Isaac and Jacob* in God's victory feast (v.11; see Psalm 107.3 on the return of Jews from all points of the compass to Jerusalem, and Isaiah 60.1–4 on the assembling of the nations to come to Jerusalem). The phrase *those who were born to the kingdom* (v.12) implies a change from the old order to the new, with the new inclusive of both Jew and Gentile. Those of the old order who refuse to recognize what God is doing in Jesus will be excluded from the kingdom altogether, and dismay and anger, *wailing and grinding of teeth*, will follow (v.12b). The language of the Old Testament covenant pattern is frequent in Matthew: blessing and curse, light and outer darkness, promised land and exile. But it is transformed in meaning as it is transferred into the new context (v.12a; see 4.16) of a world-wide people of God. (See Apocalyptic in Matthew's Gospel, pp. 148–50 below.)

The healing of Peter's mother-in-law (8.14f.) adds to the sequence of leper and Gentile the healing of a woman, but the brevity of the story, with only six verbs, only three of which have Jesus as subject, suggests that it was a tradition to be rehearsed rather than a medium for teaching about Jesus. That Jesus healed a woman may not have seemed to Matthew particularly important. It was nevertheless a significant story for a different reason; both Luke and Matthew modify the role of the male disciples, including Peter's, and the importance of the ministry of women to Jesus (see §14J) justifies its Matthean presence and form. The second half of the story reads: '*the fever left her, and she got up and attended to his needs*' (see 27.55). Matthew's gospel is often regarded as a conservative document: in it Jesus is strict and law-abiding, giving firm instructions and offering a clear example for his followers. These stories confirm suspicions that this is less than the truth. Certainly the examples are there to be followed: the humility of the centurion, the humanity of Jesus, the *diakonia* of the women. But Jesus crosses the traditional boundaries of action and expectation and his authority is of a distinctive kind, expressed in a new style of life. The final verses of the section underline this. Attached to the summary statement of his exorcisms and healings in the evening (v.16; the Marcan point that it was a sabbath end disappears in Matthew and Luke; for a biblical parallel to exorcisms see Tobit 8.1–3) is another formula quotation: Matthew 8.17, quoting Isaiah 53.4. This passage from Isaiah is translated in several different ways in modern versions, and the differences suggest the different ways in which the text can be understood. The quotation has two parts and the REB translates both parts as having the same force: '*He took away our illnesses from us and carried away our diseases.*' Jesus healed the people; he got rid of their sickness; he was renewing the wholeness of Israel (see also 9.35f. and §5A for Jesus as restorer of the people). This is a well attested translation and is currently in favour. TEV translates the first part with an alternative nuance: 'He himself took our sickness and carried away our diseases'. 'Took our sickness' is ambiguous. Does it imply that there was a cost to himself in healing others? Did the healing in 8.1–4 imply a risk: of infection and of impurity, of danger to health and to reputation? There is sufficient about the sufferings of the Son of Man in the next section (8.19) to warrant a studied ambiguity in the translation of Matthew 8.17: he removed suffering – at personal cost. His style of life is integral to his healing ministry, as is indicated later in Matthew 12.17–21, another quotation from an Isaianic Servant passage, and that style will also be a model for his disciples (10.8). But what is meant by 'sickness' and 'disease'? Not only physical maladies. For behind the stories of healing there is the purpose of God, being fulfilled in Jesus, and that purpose was described in the Prologue as opening up a new hope for the outcasts, the aliens, the dispossessed and the misjudged, revealing new horizons for Matthew's own generation. The healings are parables of renewal, renewal for the nation, for those of every nation, and for the people of God. They are powerful, allusive and encouraging stories, and at the centre of them is Jesus, the healer, who heals at a cost; and the cost of his obedience is a suffering style of life, and the isolation of his death.

B. The Migrant Son of Man
   8.18–22

8.18   *At the sight of the crowd surrounding him Jesus gave the word to cross over to the other side of the lake.* Some manuscripts heighten the pressure on Jesus by emphasizing the size of the crowd (contrast 8.18 with Mark 4.35f.). He makes the decision to cross the lake, as he does at 14.22 (where, as in Mark 6.45, he forces the disciples to embark), but there is no single motivation in Matthew for such withdrawals. In this case the decision serves an unexpected purpose: it highlights the migrant existence of Jesus. Two people consider what the decision to cross over means for them. The first, a scribe (capable in Matthew of being a disciple; see 13.52) declares his willingness to travel with Jesus wherever Jesus goes (v.19). In his answer Jesus contrasts the Son of Man with animals and birds which despite their wandering or migrant existence nevertheless are able to make homes for themselves. *'The Son of Man has nowhere to lay his head'* (v.20). The interest of the story is in the Son of Man's fate, not in the scribe's answer, although following the Son of Man in his travels might not be particularly convenient for a devout student of the law. So who is the Son of Man? The Son of Man in Matthew looks similar to the Son of Man of earlier gospel traditions: the Son of Man's authority is declared (9.6), challenged (26.2) and substantiated (26.64) as in Mark, except that in Matthew the authority to forgive (9.8) is shared more evidently with others. The Son of Man's lot is one of human loneliness and homelessness. In Luke's gospel the contrast between Son of Man and the animal kingdom is made in the context of missionary journeys. These demand incessant movement, without any seasonal breaks. They do not even allow room for farewells to one's family; they may even result in rejection or persecution. Perhaps in Matthew the reason why the Son of Man has no home is that he is given no respite by friend or foe; the crowds give him no rest, and he warns his disciples to expect the same; the lot of the Son of Man and the lot of the disciples is one and the same (see 10.25). This does not mean that the disciples and the Son of Man are indistinguishable. Far from it. The Son of Man has authority, especially over his followers. It is an authority which resides in the style of his ministry and the immediacy of his claims over those who hear and answer his call (10.24). In addition to this picture of the Son of Man, drawn from earlier traditions, there are two distinctively Matthean lines. The first establishes the Son of Man as the one who judges Israel and the nations, seated in glory (19.28; 25.31) with his angels around him (16.27); the second says that the one who will judge suffered unjustly (26.2). Like the other phrases descriptive of Jesus in Matthew, the Son of Man concentrates on Jesus the humiliated, suffering one. He suffered and continues to suffer in the agony of his own people, and of the outcasts, the aliens, the dispossessed and the misjudged (see § 13J).

8.21   *Another man, one of his disciples*, asks permission not to travel with Jesus but to go to bury his father. The answer of Jesus is uncompromising and offensive: *'Leave the dead to bury their dead'*, that is, in terms of modern speech, 'A funeral? Forget it!' Like Elijah the prophet he can require an allegiance above that of family life and duties. This does not mean that family links are irrelevant. He heals Peter's mother-in-law (8.14f.). But it does mean that the claims of discipleship must take first place (10.35–39). Nor does it mean that he attacks the law's validity. It does mean that at a time of crisis a prophet communicates through an outrageous flouting of custom and common decency.

C. A Journey by Boat
8.23–27

8.23 *Jesus then got into the boat, and his disciples followed*. Matthew now records a series of stories which in Mark and Luke appear at a later stage of the narrative. They are part of the complex assembly of material following the Sermon on the Mount. The first of them, the Stilling of the Storm (as a recent commentator Ulrich Luz suggests), betrays signs of a late version of the Marcan tradition known to both Matthew and Luke; it also resembles a later Stilling of the Storm by Jesus in 14.22–32. In both the storm is calmed; in both the focus is on divine power. In 8.23–27, immediately after the pictures of the suffering Son of Man, comes an example of power such as only God or God's agent possesses. The situation is one of greater danger, to which Jesus is oblivious (Luke omits this last feature): *All at once a great storm arose on the lake, till the waves were breaking right over the boat; but he went on sleeping* (v.24). The disciples call him 'Lord' (*kyrie*), pleading for help: 'Save us, Lord . . .'. Jesus calls the disciples cowards, those of little faith, and calms the storm. The response of the disciples is astonishment: '*What sort of man is this*?' (v.27). It is partly amazement at the raw power displayed – '*Even the wind and the sea obey him*' (v.27c) – and partly amazement at the wider sequence of events of which that demonstration of power was a part. Jesus was responsible for their being on the lake (v.18); he was the one they naturally appealed to ('*Save us, Lord; we are sinking!*', 8.25); his reaction to their panic was a reprimand: You are so anxious (see 6.30–34). Both his extraordinary power and the circumstances of their deliverance prompted their amazement. There can be little doubt that all three synoptic gospels reflected on what level of divine protection could be anticipated in great crises; the Old Testament writers did the same, whether the setting was the wilderness, or exile, or the Holy Land (see Psalm 93; Exodus 14.26f.; Isaiah 40.10–12; Jonah 2; Daniel 9.18f.; Malachi 2.17–3.5). The answer differed in different situations. In the case of Matthew 8.23–27 there was the divine presence (see 18.20; 28.20) awakening among them to still the storm, the ever-present risk of paralysing anxiety, and so to bring the people of God safely home (Isaiah 51.9–11).

D. *Acts of Mercy*
8.28–9.13

If Jesus' attitude is important in the Stilling of the Storm, the one which follows it, the Gadarene Narrative, is concerned with the attitudes of other groups to him. (Neither the Matthean name *'Gadarenes'* nor the Marcan and Lucan names 'Gerasenes' or 'Gergasenes' can be identified with any certainty – the variant manuscript readings complicate the matter further – but the setting of the story on a cliff top above the Sea of Galilee is quite clear from the narrative.) The story is far shorter in Matthew and in Luke than it is in Mark. In particular the ritual features of an exorcism fall away, and the Marcan missionary activity in the Decapolis (Mark 5.20) gives way in Matthew to Gentile rejection. In Mark there is only one demoniac; in Matthew 8.28 *Two men came to meet him from among the tombs; they were possessed by demons*. The demoniacs bar his way, and are violent ; but they find themselves confronted by someone who threatens them: *'What do you want with us? Have you come here to torment us before our time?'* (v.29). Like other demoniacs in the Jesus narratives they identify who this Jesus is: the Son of God who spells doom for all that is evil. They recognize his authority and scatter at his peremptory 'Off with you!' (v.32), carrying a distant herd of pigs over the precipice into the sea. The herdsmen and their compatriots are not unnaturally ill-disposed to him. To judge by the name Gadarene and the reference to pigs (see Leviticus 11.7) these are, according to Matthew's version, Gentiles. The story is about Gentiles who want nothing to do with Jesus. He is a disturbing character. The herdsmen scatter as their herd drowns, giving an account of the events; the whole city appeals for Jesus to go: and *when they saw him they begged him to leave the district* (v.34 : this is distinctive to Matthew). Jesus leaves them, returning to Capernaum, his home town (9.1).

At the beginning of Matthew's gospel we saw the messianic hopes of Israel being broadened and deepened. That is true here also as the healing aspect of messianic expectations is fulfilled. After all (1.6), was not Solomon, the healer, David's son! Messianic expectations included healing and wholeness, and these are taken to a new level through the narrative of the powerful Son of God. But even at the beginning of the gospel the premonitions were there of inhumanity, rejection and misunderstanding. So the cost for the obedient son is bound to be great: A Gentile city has rejected him; so also will some of the Jewish leaders. That is one feature of the next story, the Healing of the Paralytic (9.2–8). In this story Matthew continues the sequence of healings found at the beginning of Jesus' ministry according to Mark. Friends of a paralysed man have shown faith in Jesus by bringing their friend to him (v.2); he responds with a word of forgiveness: *'Take heart, my son; your sins are forgiven'* (v.3). In the subsequent debate the issue turns on how Jesus could make such a declaration. Matthew's contemporaries would have been aware of a close relationship between illness and disobedience to God. The relationship was thought of as causal in its character, to an extent virtually unknown today. The point is best illustrated by the difficulty which the book of Ecclesiasticus has in arguing for a positive role for medical doctors; they could be seen in those days as interfering with divine justice! Matthew is clear that Jesus could offer healing and forgiveness, and that he could do so because of divine authority, an authority with the power to do both. But some of the scribes rejected the claim as blasphemous: *'This man is blaspheming!'* (v.3). The power to forgive was regarded as a divine prerogative (II Chronicles 30.18f.), although it could be exercised by human agents (the Prayer of Nabonidus was, according to one of the Dead Sea Scrolls, answered by an exorcist who gave a declaration of forgiveness). The scribes' rejection of his claim was basically therefore a rejection of Jesus' claim to act on behalf of God; and this is why Jesus calls it evil: *'Why do you harbour evil thoughts?'* (v.4; and see 12.22–37). So he heals the paralysed man as a sign of his authority. But there is more to be said about authority than this. At the end of the story, instead of the people praising God for the authority granted to Jesus, they praise God *for granting such authority to men* (v.8). Why the plural, and why the general word 'people' instead of the specific name 'Jesus'? One way of throwing light on the question is to ask: Given the authority of Jesus to declare sins forgiven, how available is that forgiveness now? The narrative in 9.2–8 gives an answer: God has made forgiveness available through the agency of the Son of Man (v.6), and because of him it will be available more widely. Others, the disciples of the Son of Man in particular, will be given that authorization also.

The call of *Matthew* has provided a name for the gospel as a whole. Why the tax-collector was given the name Matthew in place of the Marcan name of Levi (Mark 2.14) is a mystery. It is important for the story that it concerned a tax-collector. The flavour of the word can be judged from traditional associations which we find in 18.17: 'treat him as you would a pagan or a tax-collector'. So whatever is concluded about Levi and Matthew, it is the traditional associations of his office which matter here, and the refusal of Jesus to be guided by them. He *said to him: 'Follow me'*. Jesus also had a meal with taxmen and sinners (v.10). He refuses to go along with the traditional view of taxmen, as the Pharisees presented it (v.11) because central to his work (according to this gospel) is the quotation from Hosea 6.6. 'I require mercy, not sacrifice'. The quotation appears in 9.13 and 12.7 (see also 5.7 and 23.23). In each case mercy is about a particular perspective on life and people. It is about not excluding others, about not condemning those who are innocent; it is about putting people above legal principles. It is about a perspective on life and the attitudes which grow from that. Jesus expressed his acceptance of sinners by eating with them, and recommends mercy as a pattern of life. Showing mercy and the experience of mercy belong together (see 5.7), as do also showing forgiveness and experiencing forgiveness. The differing attitudes to Jesus have been presented: among both Gentiles and Jews there have been those who have shown faith in Jesus; among both there have been people wanting to reject him. Critical moments are at hand.

E. New Wine and New Skins
9.14–17

Matthew recognizes fasting as an appropriate activity. Naturally for a disciple of Jesus Christ it needs to express the joy of the gospel (*'Can you expect the bridegroom's friends to be sad while the bridegroom is with them?'* 9.15a). Providing that the heart is right, fasting can be an aid to discipleship. It can express dependence on God. It can be a reminder of what it costs to follow the one who was taken by force and crucified: *'the time will come when the bridegroom will be taken away from them; then they will fast'* (9.15b). Fasting was an expression of the Jewish piety required by scripture (Leviticus 16). The disciples of John (v.14) fasted, and Jesus seems in this passage of Matthew's gospel to be approving their practice but seeking a different basis for it. The external can be preserved, as long as it relates appropriately to what is internal. 9.14f. can be read in that way. However that solution seems to be in direct contradiction with Matthew 9.16f.

9.16 says that it is no use hanging on to the old and external because what is new is bound to be destructive of it: *'No one puts a patch of unshrunk cloth on an old garment; for then the patch tears away from the garment, and leaves a bigger hole.'* The relationship between the old and the new is a subject to which Matthew keeps returning (see for example 13.52). It includes the great theme of promise and fulfilment: the old prophecies seen in relationship to the new activity of God in Jesus. In that case there is no question of dispensing with the old as if it were a piece of thin fraying cloth. The old has its honoured place: 'this had to happen so that what was spoken by the prophet might be fulfilled.' The subject of things old and new also covers the old law and its new interpretation: 'You have heard that our predecessors were told . . . But I say to you . . . ' Again, there is no question in Matthew or in Mark of dispensing with the law as if it were a stiff old wineskin. In both the law has its honoured place. Why then does Matthew retain these two pictures, the patch and the wineskin (v.17), both of which set the old over against the new? One of the more important problems with which the gospel of Matthew wrestled was the relationship between the church on the one hand and Judaism on the other. In that argument it was the new which for him had displaced the old, partly because in the new the chief actors of 9.18–38 would have a new role.

F. *Healing for the People*
9.18–36

This section concludes chs. 8 and 9. It contains four healings: the official's daughter, the woman with a haemorrhage, the two blind men, and the dumb demoniac. The first, 9.18–19, 23–26, is the restoration to life of a dead child (see I Kings 17.17–24 for Elijah raising the dead child in Zarephath). An official (it is not clear in Matthew whether his position is religious or civil) says to Jesus: *'My daughter has just died; but come and lay your hand on her, and she will live'* (v.18). In Mark the intervening story allows for a passage of time during which the child dies (Mark 5.25–35). In Matthew that function is unnecessary; the traditional funeral hubbub has already begun with hired lamenters and reed players. Jesus dismisses them all with the comment: *'she is asleep'* (v.23). The words have a double meaning: for Jesus they indicate the reversibility of death, for the official mourners an ill-mannered joke (v.24). But in response to the official's faith, and acting as Elijah did (I Kings 17.19), Jesus performs the act of restoration in private. Whether the REB is right here in v.26 and v.31 to restrict the report to the local district is questionable: the text in both places says it became the 'talk of the whole land'. Raising the dead is part of the Matthean good news and belongs with the story of Jesus (11.5; see also 9.32 and 11.15), as it does with the disciples' commission (10.8). The promise of healing for the nation is incomplete without it (Isaiah 26.19–21). Meanwhile the woman with a haemorrhage has been cured too (vv.20–22).The record, given with the utmost brevity, crosses the boundaries from normality into areas of mystery and holiness: a ritually unclean woman, believing she need only touch the fringe of his cloak, is recognized without a word being spoken, and declared whole: *'your faith has healed you'* (v.22). Next the two blind men are healed.

9.27–31   The origin of the story is linked with 20.29–34, and both appear to have developed by different routes from Mark 8.22–26. They have in common an appeal by two blind men to the healing Messiah: *'Have pity on us, Son of David!'* (v.27). They differ in one particular way. In 20.29–34 there is no specific reference to faith (contrast 20.34 and Mark 8.22–26 with Mark 10.52) whereas in 9.28 Jesus puts a direct question to blind men: *'Do you believe that I have the power to do what you want?'* to which they reply, *'We do.'* This unusual conversation marks the direction in which 9.27–31 developed and it underlines a view of faith found elsewhere in Matthew: *'As you have believed, so let it be'* (9.29; see 18.19f.; 21.22). It is a view of faith which, if it is taken out of the context of Matthew's gospel, can cause deep distress and harm. It implies that faith can achieve anything. But that of course raises the question: if a deeply desired healing does not take place, is it because of inadequate faith on the believer's part? Within the gospel it is clear that faith does not operate like that. The search for God's will is demanding and requires a sensitivity to moral issues, and a willingness to discover what the believer should request of God (26.39). Faith may work miracles through prayer; but the ultimate test, according to Matthew, is not whether the miracle or the act of healing occurs , but whether the Father's purpose is fulfilled. That is the difficult lesson to learn. It is a lesson which belongs with the question raised concerning 8.23–27: what level of protection should the believer expect? If the working of a miracle is not the ultimate test of faith, and if that is a lesson many are unwilling to learn, then vv.30f. are a singularly appropriate conclusion to a narrative about miracles and faith.

9.32f.   Finally, there is a brief note on the healing of a dumb demoniac evoking the comment: *'Nothing like this has ever been seen in Israel'* (v.33). 9.32f. resembles Matthew 12.22–24 (they are both about the healing of a dumb demoniac; see also Mark 3.22); but the closest parallel to 9.33 is in Luke 11.14, suggesting that these latter two passages represent an independent tradition, a tradition which ended with *'But the Pharisees said, "He drives out devils by the prince of devils"'* (see the REB margin at 9.33; and also Luke 11.16). So the long sequence of stories in chs. 8 to 9 culminates in a challenge to Jesus like that of 9.3, a challenge which is mentioned in 10.25 ('if the master has been called Beelzebul . . .') and which is repeated in the Beelzebul controversy (12.22–24) and in the debate about seeking for miracles and signs.

A summary follows exactly as in 4.23: what Jesus was doing was *teaching in their synagogues, proclaiming the good news of the kingdom, and curing every kind of illness and infirmity* (v.35); and to that summary is attached a fresh comment. Both the summary and the comment are fuller than in Mark (Mark 6.6,34). In Mark there is only mention of teaching and use of the language of Micaiah's prophecy in I Kings 22.17 ('like sheep without a shepherd'; see Numbers 27.17). Matthew amplifies the comment: they are 'like sheep without a shepherd, confused and exhausted'. To see the people in this state fills Jesus with pity and love. The words translated in the REB *'harassed and helpless'* have a subtle link with the descriptions earlier of those 'struck down' by illness, 'prostrate' and 'paralysed'. He meets their needs with healing, but also with the encouragement of the good news of the kingdom. Perhaps there is an implied criticism in this additional comment (see Ezekiel 34.4–6). The leadership had failed the people, leaving them vulnerable and helpless. To that extent the stories of healing again have a metaphorical aspect. Jesus is working for the 'healing of the nation' as well as for the healing of the physically and mentally ill. And that will mean confrontation with a false and unconcerned leadership which has left the people to struggle with their own problems without giving adequate help. So a new start has to be made. The task has begun; acts of healing have been witnessed; they have met with very varied results. Sometimes the reactions are antagonistic, although no one should be surprised at that. Physical healing, like the healing of a nation, can provoke opposition; it can infringe taboos and challenge deeply held convictions. The task is of monumental proportions.

§5 Mission (Discourse 2)
9.37–11.1

A. Instructions for Mission
9.37–10.25

9.37   The task is of monumental proportions. In the terms of the metaphor of the harvest, *'The crop is heavy, but the labourers too few.'* A new beginning has been made, and the fresh start will need the commissioning of labourers to continue the work. V.38 instructs disciples to pray for such a commissioning. What is prayed for in v.38 is fulfilled initially in 10.1–4. The Acts of the Apostles describes further commissions (e.g. Acts 13.1–3), and no doubt some of those who recalled the story of that first act of commissioning by Jesus would have applied the picture of the harvest to their own time. That will become evident during this chapter; some of the early Christians who rehearsed the story applied it to a strictly Palestinian mission which looked for the renewal of Israel; others found a place within such a mission for work among Gentiles; and Christians in later generations and other areas, such as those for whom Matthew wrote, took on the larger task of a world-wide harvest involving Jews and Gentiles. The comment that 'the labourers were too few' would in those situations have lost its metaphorical force; it had become a literal description: the number of workers was too small for the task.

The task is of monumental importance. It is a matter of life and death, of well-being or disaster. The proclamation of the kingdom spells hope for those who respond, and disaster for those who reject it. The commission which follows illustrates the seriousness of the task, both for the missionaries and how they approach the task, and for those who listen to them.

10.1   *Then he called his twelve disciples to him and gave them authority to drive out unclean spirits and to cure every kind of illness and infirmity.* The disciples are authorized and empowered by Jesus, named (10.2), and

64

Jesus, named (10.2), and their commission is stated (10.5). They are twelve in number, symbolizing their role in the ingathering, judging and renewing of twelve tribes of Israel (19.28). For this role they need the authority which chs. 8 and 9 have described and which the Son of Man can share with them (9.8), and the authority which Jesus will confer in 18.18.

10.2–4 calls them (for the only time in Matthew) *the twelve apostles* (see v.5), identifying the twelve with the special and privileged commission given by Jesus himself and confirmed for them at the Last Supper (26.20) and in the Great Commission (28.16 'the eleven'). Their names are given in a list shared with Mark, although with detail distinctive in Matthew (e.g. *Matthew the tax-collector*, v.3).

The commission which they are given provides one of the most difficult problems in Matthew's gospel. As a commission it is geographically limited: '*Do not take the road to gentile lands, and do not enter any Samaritan town; but go rather to the lost sheep of the house of Israel.*' To this 10.23 adds a time limitation; they are to move at high speed, fleeing from persecution; yet even so there will not be time before the Coming of the Son of Man for any wider mission than 10.5. Other parts of Matthew tell a different story. In Matthew, as in Mark, it is clearly stated that before the Parousia can happen the mission to all nations must have been completed (Mark 13.10; Matthew 24.14). Also in Matthew the Great Commission sets no limitations on missionary work except that of 'the end of time': 'Go therefore to all the nations and make them my disciples . . . I will be with you always, to the end of time' (28.19a,20). How then are these different commissions related? Perhaps 10.5 was identified with Jesus' mission (15.24); or perhaps the early tradition behind ch. 10 envisaged a strictly Palestinian mission seeking the renewal of Israel, or allowing a limited place for work among Gentiles (10.18; were Samaritans classed as Gentiles?). There were probably changes in mission strategy as Gentiles took the initiative or as the initial audience was obdurate. Whichever view of 10.5 is correct, it remains true that Matthew incorporated in the commission into ch. 10 two verses which have a narrower view of mission than the gospel as a whole. Those who take Matthew's harmonizing of his traditions to be thorough have to argue that 10.5f. belonged to the pre-Easter period and 28.18–20 to the post-Easter period. But a major difficulty stands in that way: 4.15 (see §2E) and 12.18–21 (see §6D) suggest a pre-Easter mission by Jesus as well as a post-Easter mission to Gentiles (unless these passages are turned into an imaginative prediction of world mission; and Matthew, far from indicating such an intention, quotes scripture to show that Jesus fulfilled the prophecy – he fulfilled scripture by working in Galilee of the Gentiles and proclaiming justice to the Gentiles). The seriousness of the missionary enterprise is reflected in the way the missionaries must go about their work: vv. 7f. show them following Jesus, Messiah and Lord, in the full range of Jesus' activities as seen in chs. 8–9.

10.8–10   *'Give without charge'* is what Jesus did, a principle (see II Kings 5.16) which v.10b qualifies in just one respect (see I Corinthians 9.7–10): food and lodging can be accepted. Otherwise Matthew has the strictest property rules of all the synoptic commissions (vv.9f.), leaving the missionary vulnerable and without provision for emergencies. As in the Sermon on the Mount, there is no room for anxious worries about tomorrow (see v.19).

10.11–15   concern their hosts. The missionary gives the greeting, whether the normal *'shalom'* greeting or its more specifically Christian counterpart. Whether the greeting is effective in communicating the gift of well-being or peace, depends on the warmth or coolness of the reception. Some of those visited will deserve to benefit from the greeting; others will not. The missionary is to *look for some* deserving person or house (v.11). Some will deserve the rewards involved in such hospitality (see 10.40–42) and others will not. (For the REB translations *suitable* and *welcoming* read 'deserving'; 'deserving' is a recurrent word in the passage.) The positive side of the picture is clear. But that is only part of the story. What if the host is undeserving? Failure to receive the missionary is to be answered with astonishing ferocity: the withdrawal of the greeting, abandonment of the house (*'shake the dust of it off your feet'*, v.14) and a punishment as severe as the worst corruption might warrant: *'on the day of judgement it will be more bearable for the land of Sodom and Gomorrah than for that town.'* The missionaries offer, in word and deed, as Jesus did, the stark alternatives: salvation or judgement; and the response is therefore a matter of life or death. As with Jesus, so too with the disciples, there will be a cost for them.

10.16   *'I send you out like sheep among wolves; be wary as serpents, innocent as doves.'* V.16 prepares the way for vv.17f.; missionaries are to expect legal prosecutions, public punishment, tyrannical intimidation; and, cutting even more deeply into personal confidence, family feuds, clashes between the generations, and the poignancy of family betrayal (v.21). In today's pluralist culture we are agonizingly aware of the cost to individuals who depart from their family's tradition of piety. The situation depicted in ch. 10 is a conflict of that intensity, and within it the missionary must blend wisdom with purity. But there again, there is no need for paralysing anxiety: the *'Spirit of your Father'* (v.20) will give you the words you need, and despite family treachery and public hatred there will be deliverance at the end (v.22). Jesus, the *master*, was called the devil in chief; the *pupil* or 'servant' must expect the same (vv.24f.). The humble beginnings of the disciples have never been disguised by Matthew (see §2E). Nor has their humble status. They are classed as learners, permanently. This is presented here in three different aspects: first, they are learners in the sense that they never overtake their teacher; however much they may learn they retain the status of a pupil. Later in Matthew Jesus says that they should avoid being called a teacher (23.10 'Nor must you be called "teacher"; you have one Teacher, the Messiah'). They must avoid the title for the very reason that they depend on the Teacher as the source of their teaching. Second, they are learners in the sense that what happens to their teacher will happen to them. *'The pupil should be content to share the teacher's lot'* (10.25). They must learn a way of living which includes homelessness and danger. They must learn that these are unavoidable in the course of their mission. They are one with their master and their colleagues in this (23.8). They need to develop the qualities which their teacher's lot demands and their teacher's example inspires (10.16). Third, they are can never be fully prepared for what they will have to face. The prospect is too daunting for self-confidence. But neither is it a cause for paralysing anxiety. Here again there are important reflections about the level of protection which the missionary can expect (see §4C). It is sufficient to remove anxiety; but the lesson to be learned is that the cost of mission may be the cross (10.38).

B. Four Key Issues
10.26–11.1

This section uses material shared with Luke or Mark to focus on four of the issues raised by the missionary instructions. The first begins and ends with *'Do not be afraid'* (10.26–31). Although these verses may have been formed from separate sayings they offer a single line of encouragement: behind everything stands the reality of the heavenly Father. Private instruction can become public proclamation (*'There is nothing covered up that will not be uncovered'*, v.26), physical death need hold no fears (*'Fear him rather who is able to destroy both soul and body in hell'*, v.28), because the providential care of God sustains all we are and do. (The argument is from the world as it is: *'Are not two sparrows sold for a penny? Yet without your Father's knowledge not one of them can fall to the ground'*, v.29.) That is the fundamental basis of the kingdom of Heaven from which all its values and energies proceed.

10.32f.   The second passage takes up the life and death issue of proclaiming Jesus: *'Whoever will acknowledge me before others, I will acknowledge before my Father in heaven; and whoever disowns me before others, I will disown before my Father in heaven.'* The ultimate vindication of Jesus by the Father will mean that those who take their stand with him here and now have Jesus as their advocate; the others discover him to be their judge. 'Acknowledge' and 'disown' suggest a correspondence between the two kinds of trial: the trial before councils, governors and kings and the ultimate trial before God. To disown Jesus before a human court carries its own judgement before God. There are moments in Matthew's gospel where the disciples cease to be models for Christian behaviour, and this is one of them. They disowned Jesus and the story of their failure is an integral part of the gospel. Hence the challenge here to declare allegiance to the Lord.

10.34–39   The third section reinforces the warnings of division: *'I have not come to bring peace, but a sword'* (v.34). The missionary instructions made clear that one of the significant issues which the disciple of Jesus must face is the divisiveness of religious commitments. They override personal, family and national expectations: *'No one is worthy of me who cares more for father or mother than for me'*, v.37 (see also the quotation from Micah 7.6d in v.36). The challenge is to 'take up the *cross and follow*' (v.38). The imagery of the criminal carrying the means of his execution on his own back, shamed, dishonoured, executed, an imagery deepened through the Passion story and the experience of the early church, directs the reader into the heart of the missionary task. It is the only way to life here or beyond: 'to gain life is to lose it; to lose one's life for my sake is to gain it' (v.39; see vv.32f.). There is much encouragement to be drawn here and from the Mission Discourse as a whole: that within the conflicts and the struggles of witnessing to Jesus Christ what matters above all is the reality of God and God's care.

10.40–42 There are other benefits too, called *rewards*, and they arise from the humble activities of service in the name of Christ. This concluding passage of the discourse puts them in a distinctively Matthean form: Whoever welcomes a prophet, recognizing that the prophet is one who can point to God's will and purpose in the world, will receive the blessing which belongs to a prophet's work; similarly a good person, in the same way as a prophet, has distinctive benefits of guidance and wisdom to offer. Indeed any disciple, being nothing less than a representative of God, has great riches to confer, at the cost of the simplest acts of hospitality. The challenge of the discourse is unmistakable, both to values commonly accepted in Matthew's world and to those commonly accepted in our own. All the normal notions of reward and benefit, of status or importance, are set aside. In their place come responsibilities and privileges which derive directly from the unveiling of human life and divine mercy in the life of Jesus Christ. It is in lives transformed by those values that the missionary task takes shape.

§6 Judgement and Encouragement
11.2–12.50

These chapters form an intermediate section moving from Discourse 2 (Mission) to Discourse 3 (Parables). There are many theories about its shape and function. That variety reflects the different kinds of material in chs. 11–12 and the complicated pattern of similarities in that material between Matthew, Mark and Luke. Some regard chs. 11–12 as a turning point in the gospel's story: The people of Israel have seen the Messiah's activities; yet they refuse to repent and God's judgement falls upon them. There is no doubt about the first part of that interpretation: 11.2 picks up the situation described in 4.12; John is in prison, Jesus withdraws to Galilee, settles in Capernaum, and teaches and heals in that area.

A. God's Wisdom: the Cost of Restoration
11.2–19

11.2–3b *John, who was in prison, heard what Christ was doing, and sent his own disciples to put this question to him: 'Are you the one who is to come . . .?'* There is no doubt also that Luke's gospel and Matthew's gospel have here a similar sequence of material common to them but not found in other gospels; it links the story of healings, particularly the Raising of Jairus' daughter, with John's request to Jesus about the significance of those healings (see Luke 7.1–35). But there agreement ends. The crucial issue is how to interpret 11.19. If 11.19 is about the activities of the Messiah, then 11.1–19 is about the rejection of the Messiah. If 11.19 is about both John and Jesus then the initial Matthean passage in 11.2–19 (parallel to Luke 7.18–35) is about the rejection of both John and Jesus; v.19 is about the activities of God's wisdom (v.19 is better translated 'So God's wisdom is vindicated by its activities'), and the immediately preceding verses (vv.16–19) show that those activities involve contrasting styles of life. Both

70

John and Jesus are expressions of God's wisdom; they are very different but they are nevertheless both rejected. The pattern is familiar for those who know Wisdom literature. Wisdom is God's purpose (Wisdom 9.1), expressed in creation, in the law (Wisdom 6.18), in holy men and women, in prophets, in their thoughts, words and actions, in teaching about the seasons and epochs, about the gentle ordering of all things and the deliverance of God's people and miraculous events (Wisdom 7.7–8.1); but Wisdom is ignored and disaster, indiscipline, corruption, tyranny and idolatry result (Wisdom 10.8), and suffering for God's friends and agents, who in the end experience divine help and deliverance. 11.19 belongs within that tradition, and reflects on the varied nature of God's wisdom and the fate of God's friends and agents. 11.20–30 has similar links with the Wisdom tradition, and later comments on this chapter will indicate the importance of this strand of Matthean material (see also 10.40–42).

11.2–6   At the beginning of the chapter John the Baptist sends disciples to ask if Jesus is the Coming One (see 3.7–12, 'the one who will baptize with the Holy Spirit and with fire'). The answer which they receive is threefold: first, Jesus points by way of a reply to acts of healing which correspond with the earlier summaries and narratives of what Jesus had been doing (4.24; 8.16; 9.35; see also 13.16f.); second, the acts of healing are listed in the third person ('*the blind recover their sight, the lame walk, lepers are made clean*'), so that they include also what Jesus authorized the disciples to perform (10.1); third, there is a beatitude in 11.6, translated in the REB, '*blessed are those who do not find me an obstacle to faith.*' It is difficult to give a precise meaning to this beatitude, but an example of the 'obstacle' mentioned in v.6 is the attitude of the Pharisees in 9.34 and 12.24: they attributed the exorcisms of Jesus to the prince of devils rather than to the Spirit; they refused to see God at work in Jesus; they found in Jesus an obstacle to faith in that sense. Actually the words 'to faith' in that translation are an explanatory phrase added by the translators, and because of a traditional meaning of 'faith' as 'Christian belief' could lead to a misunderstanding of 11.6. The positive form of the statement, 'blessed are those who', could be understood, in line with ch.12, as a blessing on those who witness Jesus' activities and who do not ascribe them to Satan but recognize their origin in the work of God's Spirit. That is, of course, to make a distinction between Jesus and the Holy Spirit, between the one who is agent and the originating power. God's Spirit in Matthew's gospel often seems, like the Spirit in the Eastern Fathers of the Church such as John Chrysostom, to be a powerful and holy mystery (see 'the Spirit of your Father' in 10.20). Jesus heals by the Spirit (12.15–21, 28) and that emphasizes the mysterious nature of the kingdom which he proclaims and of which he is a divinely begotten and authorized agent (1.18–20; 3.16). Agent and originating power are distinguished in Matthew, and the distinction can be illustrated in many different ways. For example 'spirit' has for Matthew transcendent associations; there is less interest in Matthew than in Mark in 'unclean spirits' (they are often called 'demons' in Matthew), presumably because to call them 'spirits' would be to accord them a false significance. 11.6, *'blessed are those who do not find me an obstacle to faith'* could therefore imply a distinction between Jesus and the Spirit, a distinction of the kind made explicit in 12.31f.: to find offence in what Jesus does may not be so ultimately catastrophic as vilifying the Spirit. But, says 11.6, there is nevertheless a blessing for those who see *'the blind recover their sight, the lame walk, the lepers . . . made clean, the deaf hear, the dead . . . raised'*, and good news brought to the poor, and who recognize that there in Jesus God is at work. In its context then 11.6 may refer to a particular offence which could be taken at this agent of the Spirit; as an answer to John the Baptist it might refer to those who expect the agent of the Spirit to come primarily as a refining fire, or, at the very least, not with the humility and gentleness of a healer and renewer. There is a blessing for those who recognize God at work in all that Jesus does.

11.7–14 The problem is, as the following verses indicate, that divine activity of every kind can be misinterpreted or misunderstood. That was true of the work of Jesus and of his disciples; it was also true of John as forerunner and herald. The proper evaluation of John is the subject of vv.7–14. It is fourfold: First, in vv.7–9 Matthew picks up a tradition about John the Baptist which establishes his claim to be *'far more than a prophet'*. It is one of the earliest datable traditions in the gospels, with an implied and uncomplimentary reference to Herod Antipas and the latter's use of a common reed on coinage before 28 CE (*'a reed swaying in the wind'* v.7). Matthew would no doubt have been unaware of that historical reference, although the association between unreliability and royal finery, and between prophetic strength and asceticism would have had considerable appeal (v.8). Like Luke, Matthew notes the claim of John to be more than a prophet and supports it with a quotation from Exodus 23.20, *'Here is my herald, whom I send ahead of you'*, and from Malachi 3.1, *'he will prepare your way before you'* (v.10). But unlike Luke, Matthew relates the prophecy of a preparatory messenger to the coming Elijah (11.14) just as Malachi 4.5 does. John is parallel to the prophets, not least in his suffering role; as Wisdom suffers rejection, so the prophets like Elijah and Jeremiah are rejected also. John is parallel to the prophets but he is far more than a prophet, because he fulfils the prophetic role to which Elijah and Jeremiah pointed; he announces God's anticipated restoration and renewal of the covenant (see Matthew 17.9–13).

Second, in v.11 Matthew, like Luke, restates this eminence of John the Baptist in general terms (*'no one has been greater than John'* 11.11a) but then qualifies it: *'and yet the least in the kingdom of Heaven is greater than he'* (11.11b). This cautionary word about John can hardly mean that he has no part in the kingdom; 11.12 says specifically, *'Since the time of John the Baptist the kingdom of Heaven has been subjected to violence.'* His work is part of the kingdom. In what sense then is John least in the kingdom? Perhaps this is another of the contexts where Matthew has failed to tie up all the loose ends. His tradition spoke of John as least, and the tradition is allowed to speak for itself. Matthew might of course mean that, although John has a part in the kingdom, he does not share in the main privilege of those who are least, that of being identified with Jesus: 'anything you did for one of my brothers here, however insignificant, you did for me' (25.40). Alternatively, in the light of 11.29, Matthew might have understood v.11 as a criticism of John: martyr he may have been, but he and his message lacked the dimension of gentleness, and that made John's yoke hard to bear.

Third, in v.12, one area of John's pre-eminence is emphasized again: he was the first to suffer from *'violent men'* who *'are taking it by force'* (11.12c). Many translations of this verse have been offered and many suggestions made about the identity of the 'violent men' (Herod, Pharisees and Sadducees, political activists, evil forces, or even impatient or importuning disciples). But there is no need to decide between all these alternatives. If Herod was the one who had John executed, he was only one of the many tyrants, rulers and leaders who continued the persecution (10.17–20). Fourth, John differed from Jeremiah and Elijah in that he belonged to the time which they could only envisage (v.13); he was part of the fulfilment (*'the destined Elijah'*) and fulfilment is, in part, what defines the kingdom. According to Matthew's material those four elements provide a proper evaluation of John.

The close relationship between John the Baptist and Jesus has been stressed (see §2A) : there is so much which links them, not least that they were both subjected to petulant criticism. The works which God had been doing in both of them were misunderstood. It required discrimination to recognize God's ways (and still does, v.15), and discriminating judgement was missing. They had very different life-styles (vv.16–19), different qualities of life, and different roles. But it made no difference to the people around them who they were or what they did. The works of God were misinterpreted or dismissed, of whatever kind they were. People found an excuse to dismiss them both. Yet they were both expressions of divine wisdom. Different though they were, both John and Jesus were in their distinct ways forms of divine activity and vindications of how God works (11.19). In what sense they are vindications of how God works will become apparent in the next few sections.

B. *Judgement on Three Towns*
11.20–24

The works of God witnessed by the cities of Galilee become now a decisively new context for the common proclamation of John the Baptist and Jesus. Jesus has been teaching and healing in the towns and villages of Galilee (4.23); his mission has also been broadened to include the whole nation (9.32f.). Like John he has been proclaiming: 'Repent, for the kingdom of Heaven is upon you!' His mission of preaching and healing has spread far and wide. Earlier the people have been described as harassed and helpless. Now it is implied in vv.20–24 that they are unrepentant. Despite all the preaching and healing, repentance has not happened. This new situation is expounded by means of two fierce contrasts. The first contrast is between two little-known Galilean villages and two famous Gentile cities. Words of judgement were spoken on Tyre and Sidon by the Old Testament prophets, yet the two Gentile cities are said to be more easily brought to repentance than the Galilean villages. They would have responded more vigorously to Jesus' mission than Galilee has (vv.21f.). The second contrast is between Jesus' own home town (Capernaum, see 9.1) and the most notorious place in the biblical tradition, Sodom. Capernaum is characterized by means of another allusion to an Old Testament prophet, this time very specific. Isaiah had prophesied that Babylon's pride would be its downfall. Jesus applies those very words to Capernaum. Its pride would be its downfall. The two contrasts are fierce, and the condemnation wholesale and unqualified. Jesus sounds like an Old Testament prophet, but he stresses the significance of this generation. This generation has far less excuse than those the prophets addressed. This generation's responsibility will be greater (v.24), presumably because Jesus' coming marks the period of fulfilment; and the judgement on them will be correspondingly severe.

These contrasts do not make for easy reading. They are hard to reconcile with pictures of Jesus as the forgiving friend of sinners and with the dimension of gentleness to be found at the end of ch.11. But the problem which Jesus identifies in Capernaum's case is a serious matter; repentance is required and repentance is possible, but when people assume for themselves a position of privilege, repentance becomes more and more unlikely. Self-satisfaction dulls the conscience. Fierce and uncompromising criticism is then a measure of true concern and care.

C. *Encouragement for the People*
11.25–30

Matthew presents John the Baptist and Jesus as sharing the same message and a similar fate. They are both expressions of the divine wisdom. Different though they are, they are agents of the one wisdom. They represent the one God. Jesus does so particularly as a teacher of wisdom, teaching what the Father has revealed (11.25–27; compare Luke 10.21f.). He offers God thanksgiving for the insights he has received (see Ecclesiasticus 51.1–23), for hiding them from the wise (see I Corinthians 1.19; Isaiah 29.14) and revealing them to the simple few (v.25 ; see Ecclesiasticus 3.20; 6.22; 51.23). His address is to the '*Father, Lord of heaven and earth*'. That relationship to the universal God is explored through the relationship of father and son, in which the sharing of the father's heart and mind is a privilege enjoyed by the son, and through the son by a chosen few (v.27). It is a gracious act of divine wisdom (v.26). So he is able to speak with wisdom's voice. He encourages people to listen and respond (11.29f.; see Ecclesiasticus 51.23–30), pointing to the ultimate benefits of the strenuous efforts required: '*Come to me, all who are weary and whose load is heavy; I will give you rest*' (v.28). But Jesus is more than a teacher of wisdom. He embodies wisdom in the sense that he illustrates obedience and humility in the way that he teaches. He illustrates it by the way he lives: '. . . *learn from me, for I am gentle and humble-hearted.*' He not merely teaches that the humble in heart will be blessed. He is himself humble of heart (v.29). Responsive to the Father, he sets the pattern for all God's children. In contrast with the pride of Capernaum he offers a different and more costly way. The parallels here with Ecclesiasticus are strong ('*My yoke is easy to wear*'; see Ecclesiasticus 6.24–31). It is true that there are also hints in this section of Jeremiah's prophecy (especially of Jeremiah 6.16 'You will find rest for yourselves') and of Jeremiah's hope that prophetic suffering will prepare the way for a restoration of the people of God. But what makes the Wisdom tradition so crucial for ch.11 is the link between the rejection of wisdom and of the pattern of life which wisdom encourages. The way of Jesus, apparently costly and demanding at first sight, opens up for those who listen a way of healing and release. So a clue to God's way of working is the responsiveness that goes with humility. That is one reason why God's wisdom is vindicated by its results; it establishes a pattern which makes the fulfilment of the divine purpose realizable. This is what is revealed in God's Son, in this strangely humble Messiah. Wisdom enables us to explore that revelation, its universal character and authority, and the form of practical living which it affirms for all, Jew and Gentile alike. Wisdom therefore suggests one way in which the writer of the gospel viewed the relationship of Jesus to God. The nature of that relationship and of that revelation is glimpsed in ch.11 through wisdom language. It is seen in other ways in the following chapters. Presented in different ways it remains a continuing interest of the gospel.

D. *The Compassionate Servant*
12.1–21

12.1 *About that time Jesus was going through the cornfields on the sabbath.* Matthew shares with Mark two stories about the sabbath: the Disciples in the Cornfields and the Healing on the Sabbath. In Matthew they illustrate one further way in which the yoke of Christ is lighter. With other teachers of his day Jesus brought a humanitarian concern to the interpretation of the law, especially to interpretation of the sabbath laws (Matthew 12.1–8, 9–14). Human compassion directs how the law may be understood. Compassion for the hungry can override ritual regulations; compassion for an animal can override restrictions on sabbath movements or work (12.11). In both cases scripture provides the warrant for the exceptions. Scripture itself authorizes compassion: '*It is mercy I require, not sacrifice*' (v.7; see §4D). There is however another side to Matthew's story of the Disciples in the Cornfields. In Mark Jesus answers the Pharisees by quoting what David did, presumably on the sabbath, '*when he and his men were hungry*'. (I Samuel 21.1–6), and Matthew repeats this humanitarian response: '*He went into the house of God and ate the sacred bread*' (v.4), an act '*forbidden*' by law (Leviticus 24.5–9). But Matthew adds: '*Or have you not read in the law that on the sabbath the priests in the temple break the sabbath and they are not held to be guilty?*' (v.5; see Numbers 28.9f.). That example from scripture provides a different kind of basis for action; it is not now a matter of compassion for the hungry taking precedence over ritual require- ments: it is where one ritual responsibility is given precedence over another. The discussion of ritual responsibilities remains important. Scripture did not allow work on the sabbath (Exodus 20.10), but the regulations encouraged a host of questions: What constituted work? Deuteronomy 23.25 might suggest that rubbing plucked corn in your hands did not, and therefore the disciples, if that is what they did, had not contravened the sabbath law. And what constituted work which could take precedence over the sabbath law? That latter question exposes a factor in Matthew's material which was not present in Mark's: the need to take account of the arguments of the legal rigorists. Some argue that 24.20 carries a similar concern: flight on the sabbath would have been unacceptable to some and account would have to be taken of their views. But unacceptable to whom? To Jews? Not all Jews would have taken such a firm line: Josephus gives an account of a Jewish sabbath escape (Josephus, *Wars* 4.97–111). Or was it unacceptable in relationships between Jews and Christians? And what were the relationships between Jews and Christians in Matthew's day, and would Christians have adapted their regula- tions to suit local Jews? Or was it unacceptable specifically to Jewish Christians? In the latter case it would certainly have been a special group of legalist Jewish Christians, since for some Jewish Christians ritual requirements became of secondary importance; certainly that was the case after the fall of the Jerusalem temple. Matthew's material seems to have taken such considerations into account (see 5.18–20), and 12.5 may be an illustration of that. So Matthews' material may take account of the legal rigorist position, and of a legalist position held by some Christians. But that is true only to a limited extent. Vv.6f. continue: *'But I tell you, there is something greater than the temple here. If you had known what this text means, "It is mercy I require . . ."'* Important though the temple discussion may be, scripture still gives precedence to mercy. Moreover scripture has to be applied in this case to a distinctive situation (vv.7f.): to the disciples required by the Son of Man to take up his wandering pattern of life (8.18–22), with no emergency rations (10.10), in order to proclaim with all speed the message which the Son of Man has given them (10.7). That qualifies them to be regarded as *'innocent'* before the law (v.7), for the Son of Man's requirements take precedence, even over sabbath law (v.8, *'For the Son of Man is lord of the sabbath'*). The argument in Matthew is in some ways different from Mark's argument (Mark 2.23–28): Mark has no reference to priestly sabbath duties, only to the precedent for doing on the sabbath what was ritually forbidden; and Mark highlights the function of the law in enabling God's will for humanity to be fulfilled (Mark 2.27); as Matthew does in 12.12. What Matthew and Mark have in common is that both recognize the circumstances which are special to those who follow Jesus. For them Jesus was not a destroyer of the Jewish law; however old rules could no longer apply as they did. That is also the case with the healing of the man *with a withered arm* (v.10). The question is raised: *'Is it permitted to heal on the sabbath?'* (v.11), and the answer is given that humanitarian concern, for animals and therefore for human beings, ought to be served and not thwarted by the sabbath regulations (v.12).

This is the first focus of Pharisaic opposition to Jesus in ch.12; they oppose his attitude to the sabbath. The events are seen as part of a plot *to bring a charge against* Jesus (v.10b) and they result in the decision of the Pharisees to destroy him (v.14). Jesus withdraws again, accompanied by many followers. There are further healings (v.15) which conclude with the comment: *He gave strict instructions that they were not to make him known* (v.16) – the theme of secrecy. In Mark the theme of secrecy enfolds something of the mystery of God's work in Christ: The seed growing secretly, the message which is hidden from some and revealed to others, Christ silent before the high priest – all these illustrate the distinctiveness of Mark's gospel message. As we have seen, in Matthew the theme of secrecy is treated less uniformly, and it is understood here by means of a quotation from Isaiah about God's servant. Part of that quotation reads: *He will not strive, he will not shout, nor will his voice be heard in the streets* (12.19). This is the servant's secret way, his humble demeanour, his avoidance of show. The quotation continues: *He will not snap off a broken reed, nor snuff out a smouldering wick . . .* (12.20). This too belongs to the servant's secret way: a gentleness with the weak and the unpromising. The theme of secrecy in Matthew focuses on undervalued qualities of life and behaviour. But alongside these gentle qualities is a complementary motif: the motif of justice – *He will proclaim justice among the nations* (12.18), and *until he leads justice on to victory. In him the nations shall put their hope* (vv.20f.). There is a revolution of world proportions in this servant's vocation. Hidden within the humility of the servant is a massive potential which will uproot the tyrant and avenge innocent blood.

E. The Beelzebub Controversy
12.22–36

The second focus for Pharisaic opposition in ch.12 is the healing of a blind and dumb demoniac (vv.22f.) and the crowd's association of Jesus with the name 'David's Son': *'Can this be the Son of David?'* The Pharisees reassert their view that Jesus can only be casting out demons by the higher authority of the *prince of devils* (v.24), and Jesus, presented in the narrative as fully aware of the debate, takes up their debate in the form of parables. 'Prince' suggests a *kingdom* (v.25); higher authority suggests a diversity of policy and vision, perhaps a disintegrating diversity: *A kingdom divided against itself is laid waste* (v.25). Jesus picks up the Pharisaic picture of absolute authority and exposes its other side: the desolation of revolt and civil war. The realism of the picture is underlined by the phrase *is laid waste*. The picture is also of a kingdom working with its laws, affiliations, honour and commitments, and Jesus allows the hearer to reflect on how such kingdoms are exclusive of each other. To place Jesus in the wrong kingdom is a calamitous mistake. The two kingdoms – of Satan, of God – are exclusive of each other, and the Matthean context gives force to this in the statements about Pharisaic opposition and the plot to kill Jesus.

12.25 The parables then become more local, first reducing the perspective to the town and then to the household. The more local they become, the more poignant, petty and personally destructive are the implications. V.26 underlines this; it is phrased in the most ironical and ridiculous terms: it is not a matter of Satan casting out demons, but of *Satan who drives out Satan*. Satan is a divided self. An important shift takes place. The confrontion is now between kingdoms, one of which is inherently incapable of maintaining itself: *how then can his kingdom stand?* (v.26) The conflict within Satan's kingdom is underlined by a further comment: they attribute Jesus' exorcisms to Satan but in the case of the Pharisaic exorcisms they do not (v.27). How contradictory their judgements have become! Jesus then comes to his view of the matter. Suppose after all it is God's Spirit at work in his healings; then exorcisms are a sign of the kingdom's presence, and the Pharisees have called this 'Satan' (v.28). An additional picture supports the statement: to control or dispose of a strong man's property requires an invasion of the kind already mentioned in v.28. The conflicting forces for and against Jesus are earnestly engaged (v.30). They are locked in combat, with the kingdom of evil already doomed through internal strife. By means of the three parables Jesus denies the charge, and then faces his critics with the ultimate question. There is a chasm opening up in front of them. Not only is the charge nonsensical: Satan would not destroy his own powers; it is also blasphemous; those who make it will discover that they are slandering God to his face, and the penalty for that is unthinkable. The Son of Man may appear weak and vulnerable; not so the divine strength operating in him (vv.31f.): *if anyone speaks against the Holy Spirit, for him there will be no forgiveness*. All this may sound unrelated to everyday life. But it is characteristic of Matthew's gospel to bring together the massive issues of world significance and issues of day to day living. That is the case here. The critics of Jesus are risking the unthinkable; they are calling God evil to his face. But in fact this comes down to the practical matters of language and speech. Words betray the reality of what is in the heart. Foolish and blasphemous charges would not have been made if the whole person were not rotten to the core. *Good people from their store of good produce good; and evil from their store of evil produce evil* (v.35). So, concludes Jesus, at this most practical of levels, *Out of your own mouth you will be acquitted; out of your own mouth you will be condemned* (v.37). What makes possible this link between the universal and the everyday is the reality of judgement. What is said may have the ring of exaggeration about it: *every thoughtless word you speak you will have to account for on the day of judgement* (v.36). But the exaggeration makes a real point. In terms of human responsibility before God what we say, do and write matters; their implications spread far beyond any one immediate time and place.

F. Rebukes to an Evil Generation
12.37–50

The final section of this chapter, again involving the Pharisees (with some scribes), has three parts, each of which recalls an earlier part of the gospel. It is as if Matthew had several particular interests and the narratives reflect now one, now the other. The first recalls the fierce contrasts of 11.20–24 where Jesus stated that Gentile towns would have reacted more favourably to his mission than Israelite towns. This time the point is made in a slightly different way. There are two contrasts again. The first is that the ancient pagan city of Nineveh repented when Jonah warned them of God's judgement (v.41). By contrast this '*godless generation*', faced with a greater opportunity and in greater danger of judgement, neglects the signs that have been given them: Jonah, as a sign to them of resurrection and prophetic power (v.40); the Ninevites, as a lasting rebuke (v.41). The second contrast is gentler: the Queen of Sheba took great care to discover Solomon's wisdom; she too is a permanent rebuke to this generation and will be so at the end (v.42).

12.43–45   The second part of this final section is a kind of fable. It continues the earlier discussion about expecting bad fruit from bad trees. It has the same general message as a fable such as the Fox and the Hedgehog: 'Get rid of one, and the rest will arrive, all hungry!' Jesus is saying: Get rid of one evil spirit and the rest will soon arrive, all of them eager to take up residence. The point is simple: Unless you build up the qualities of Christian living (watching your language, cultivating a receptive frame of mind, discovering the power of humility, and taking up your cross) you will be under continual threat from the powers of evil.

The third story is a disconcerting episode; Jesus makes the Father's will the key test of close relationships. Earlier Jesus had warned that he had not come to bring peace but a sword, and that a person's enemies would come from the family and household. Now he uses family relationships to examine the new relationships which commitment to the Father's revelation will forge (v.48). As the mission of Jesus demands of the disciples that they should leave their homes and relatives, it also provides a new kind of family and a new set of personal loyalties: *'Here are my mother and my brothers. Whoever does the will of my heavenly Father is my brother and sister and mother'* (see Matthew 19.29).

§7 Parables (Discourse 3)
13.1–53

A. Failure and Success (the Sower)
13.1–23

Chapter 13, the chapter of parables, lacks a clear structure. Like Mark 4 it presents parables which challenge the hearer to respond to the message of the kingdom. But perhaps even more than Mark, Matthew 13 gives weight to the contrast between the privilege of hearing the good news and possible failures in response. The Parable of the Sower in Matthew 13.3–9 illustrates the point well. Teaching from a boat by the lakeside (v.1) with the crowd on the shore (v.2), Jesus begins a sequence of parables (v.3) with the Sower. The sower scatters seed, some *along* or beside the *footpath*, some *on rocky ground*, some *among thistles* and some *on good soil*. The first three fail at different stages of growth, and whereas the parable ends in Mark with an ascending scale of success, Matthew's version ends with the law of diminishing returns: the *good soil . . . produced a crop, some a hundredfold, some sixtyfold, and some thirtyfold*. It is as if the story is saying: the possibility of a rich harvest is there; but take care that it does not turn into a failure. The responsibility is yours (v.9). That opening picture fits with the strange answer which is given concerning the purpose of parables (v.10): the disciples come to Jesus (disturbing the scene set in vv.1–3 and assumed again in vv 34f.) and ask, '*Why do you speak to them in parables?*' The parables are addressed to all, as the seed is cast widely; they provide a rich opportunity for the committed few to grasp the revelation which the Son of God has brought, just as the good soil produces a harvest (13.11; see 11.25). This is a privilege which brings with it increasing opportunities for the committed few (v.12: *For those who have will be given more*), but eventual failure for the rest. So that is why parables are for everyone (v.13a: *That is why I speak to them in parables*); the result so often is failure (v.13b: *they look without seeing*), which is what Isaiah said would happen (vv.14–15a); the people will not and cannot hear what God has to say.

In Mark 4 the people concerned may be, as in Isaiah's time, the people of Israel; it is as if the only possible excuse why Israel would not hear the good news must be a permanent (God-inflicted?) deafness. In Matthew 13 the reference may be in part the same; but it extends to all who will not listen, whether Jew or Gentile. The failure of the people to hear only discloses part of the purpose of parables. Part of their purpose, it is true, is to present the good news in a form which the hearers can reject. They do not force the truth on the hearers. But the parables are also an opportunity for genuine hearing, for repentance. In Matthew the quotation from Isaiah ends differently from in Mark (although the REB does not make this clear). The purpose of the parables holds out the possibility that some may hear, repent and change their ways: *Otherwise*, (or better 'Maybe'; see the same construction and sense in II Tim 2.25) *their eyes might see, their ears hear, and their minds understand, and then they might turn to me, and I would* (or better 'shall') *heal them* (v.15; see 13.54). The parables are an opportunity for that to happen, for the crowd to hear; their form encourages a freedom of response. It may be a fruitless freedom. It might on the other hand be the beginning of penitence. Nevertheless, continues Matthew 13 in its presentation of the purpose of parables, whatever the people's response may be, the disciples, and those few committed to seeking God's way (vv.16f.), have an unparalleled privilege, one which carries with it an unparalleled responsibility.

13.18–23   The interpretation of the Sower is then addressed specifically to the disciples: *Hear then the parable of the sower* (v.18). It is addressed to them as part of the teaching they themselves must give to others (28.20); it is also practical advice for the sustaining of their own commitment. As in Mark and Luke the concern is particularly that external pressures such as persecution and threats or competing attractions and anxieties might cause failure. Among these pressures money is named. Matthew, like Mark, warns against the *false glamour of wealth* (v.22 REB), which is a major concern of the gospel. Luke's interpretation of the Sower asks for perseverance through trials and tribulations. Matthew's emphasis is on the growth of Christian commitment through the demands of missionary work, and in line with the previous chapter, on the qualities of life and action which those who are committed need to develop (13.23). Again, as in the parable (although the interpretation of the parable and the parable itself do not always exactly match in Matthew's gospel), the warning note is sounded again at the end: *a hundredfold, or sixtyfold, or thirtyfold*.

B. *Judgement Awaits Everyone (the Darnel)*
13.24–43

The audience for the next group of parables is not defined: *Here is another parable he gave them* (v.24). It might be assumed that 'them' refers to the disciples; however v.34 describes what is happening as *teaching to the crowds . . . in parables*, in fulfilment of the promise that divine secrets will be declared in parables (v.35, quoting Psalm 78.2). Moreover one of the parables included at this point is provided with an interpretation specifically for the disciples; it is given at their request, later in the chapter (vv.36–43). So presumably the parable itself and the group of other parables with it were part of public parabolic teaching, and, like the seed widely sown, gave all an opportunity to make a response, unveiling the truth of God for those who could see. The problem of evil dominates the parable of the Darnel (13.24–30) and its interpretation (13.36–43). The parable itself is the story of a sower who discovered that *darnel* had been sown among his *good seed* (vv.25f.). It takes the initial story of the Sower a stage further. In the initial story it is the quality of the ground which affects the result. In this story it is the quality of the seed; darnel is sown among the wheat, which can only be dealt with at harvest time: *'Gather the darnel first, and tie it in bundles for burning; then collect the wheat into my barn'* (v.30). At the simplest level the parable raises new questions about why poor harvests happen, and why and to what extent the sower's work is frustrated. An enemy is at work (v.28): That statement stimulates the basic questions: evil forces are at work trying to frustrate the work of God – what is their role and fate? The answer is that their fate is already sealed. Alongside the parable of the Darnel are two other parables about growth, the Mustard Seed (vv.31f.) and the Yeast (v.33), both of which use exaggeration to suggest the mighty possibilities hidden in tiny beginnings. They encourage the faint-hearted to believe against evidence to the contrary, that God is working his purpose out. When the scene shifts to private explanations in the house (v.36), the interpretation of the

Darnel provides a series of equations: '*The sower of the good seed is the Son of Man. The field is the world; the good seed stands for the children of the kingdom, the darnel for the children of the evil one, and the enemy who sowed the darnel is the devil. The harvest is the end of time, and the reapers are angels*' (vv.37–39).

13.41–43   The explanation is however unclear at a vital point: what is meant by the angels of the Son of Man *gathering out of his kingdom every cause of sin, and all whose deeds are evil*? Is v.41 about the world or about the community of believers, the church? One clear answer can be given: whichever of the two options we choose, that option has consequences which, in strictly literal terms, do not fit with other parts of Matthew's gospel. Choose 'the world' and the idea of the Son of Man gathering from an earthly kingdom does not fit with the Son of Man bringing in a heavenly kingdom (16.28), nor does it fit with the notion of a restricted mission (10.5); choose 'the church' and the idea of leaving everything to *the end of time* (v.40) conflicts with the church discipline of 18.15–17. Either way the hearer is left with some hard thinking to do. Against the background of a world-wide mission the problem of conflicting moral standards needs to be faced; 'evil deeds' need to be judged by Jew and Gentile with comparable criteria. Against the background of church discipline the problem of universal judgement needs to be faced; who is judged at the last day and are there 'righteous' (v.43) outside the church? An attempt is made to meet some of these questions in the Sheep and the Goats (25.31–45; see §9B). At this point we are left, perhaps by design, with unanswered questions. Above all we are left with the question about the time of evil's demise. We have already seen that some think that the writer of Matthew saw God and Satan as competing powers, while others recognize that for Matthew the kingdom of Heaven is about the sole and supreme responsibility of God. Certainly in the previous chapter Satan's kingdom was divided and broken. Evil however is powerful, taking many forms, and many safeguards have to be built into the lives of disciples to counter its effects. Disciples need to develop qualities of Christ-like living; they need patterns of corporate discipline. So the parable of the Darnel raises questions which are practical as well as theoretical, and the parables contribute important elements to the debate. The Old Testament quotation in v.35 treats the parables as revelation, as a disclosure of what has been 'kept secret since the world was made'. What is now revealed is the sharing of God's supreme sovereignty

sovereignty with his authorized representative, his beloved Son (v.41), the same Son of Man who is responsible for sowing and harvesting (see § 9 A).

C. *The Old and the New (the Scribe)*
13.44–53

The Sermon on the Mount introduced us to an important feature of Matthew's gospel: strenuous efforts are required, but always against a background of fresh opportunities being offered. That is true of the whole of ch. 13, especially of the three parables in vv.44–50. The language of the parable of the Treasure hints at the strenuous efforts necessary to take advantage of the kingdom's privileges. There is a level at which the kingdom has to be won. Perhaps that level includes the commerce to which the parable alludes. On the other hand the finding of a buried treasure has usually something of the fortuitous about it. It is by no means entirely a matter of effort and struggle. The same can be said of the parable of the Pearl. It is akin to the saying about 'the one who seeks will find' (7.7); a merchant searching for a pearl is eventually rewarded by the richest find of all. The last of the parables resembles the parable of the Darnel. The Net opens up again the fearsome character of rejection. The *wicked* will be separated *from the good*, and the emphasis is (as it was in John the Baptist's preaching) on *the blazing furnace* and the *grinding of teeth*. The section ends with Jesus' question: *'Have you understood all this?'* They give an affirmative answer. They are not outright failures, whatever mistakes they may make. Indeed without their understanding we should lack a testimony to all that Jesus taught. Jesus' reply in v.52 is rather like a riddle, and half the fun of a riddle is making up your mind how to understand it. It is a riddle about one of Matthew's favourite themes: the old and the new. Can you make sense of what God has done and is now doing? Can you make sense of what you have been taught and are now being taught, of the old law and Jesus' new interpretation? Well, if you can then you deserve the name of a 'discipled scribe'!

§8 Rejection and Miracles
13.54–16.12

A. Jesus and his Family
13.54–58

After the Parables Discourse (13.53: *When Jesus had finished these parables*) Matthew takes up again the sequence of stories as it appears in Mark. Jesus returns to Nazareth (13.54) and is rejected there (an event to which Luke 4.16, 22–24, 28–30 also refers;see also John 4.44). Although elsewhere he is treated as a prophet, his own home town takes offence. All begins well: *he taught the people in their synagogue. In amazement they asked* (v.54) *'Where does he get this wisdom from, and these miraculous powers?'* But then his home town fails to square the extraordinary character of his words and deeds with the ordinary circumstances of his birth. Those ordinary circumstances are presented by Matthew in an intriguing form (vv.55f.): he is son of *the carpenter* (it is not clear whether Mark had that precise phrase); his mother is *called Mary* (perhaps the least problematic way of presenting the fact); he has brothers and sisters (some of their names are repeated elsewhere as children of a different Mary; see 27.56). But however problematic and intriguing the phrases may be, they suggest ordinary home circumstances, incompatible as far as the inhabitants of Nazareth are concerned with a prophetic manner and reputation. So they take offence (v.57; see 11.6): REB *they turned against him.* The proverb *'A prophet never lacks honour except in his home town . . .'* (v.57) is well attested in the traditions about Jesus (see John 4.44; Gospel of Thomas 31), and reveals interestingly his high reputation elsewhere. Nazareth is presented as the exception: only there *he did not do many miracles . . . such was their want of faith* (v.58). The point is an important one. Some read Matthew's gospel as a progressive turning of the Jewish people against Jesus, and treat this story as illustrative of general and increasing opposition. That is not in fact what the story says. What it does say is to confirm Jesus' high reputation, to reiterate the distinction between the ordinary history of Jesus and the wisdom and power God gives him, and to stress the association between miracles and faith (see 9.29).

B. John the Martyr
14.1–12

The Baptist's death is a paradigm of the fate of the righteous, and evidence of the villainy of kings and princes. His death is reported to Jesus (v.12). Just as the disciples of John earlier had acted as messengers between the Baptist and Jesus, so now they bring him the news of John's martyrdom. However the story begins with Jesus, and it ends with Jesus also. It opens with Herod identifying Jesus as a resurrected John. This for Herod explains the powerful acts of Jesus (v.2). In this way the narrative hints that the fate of John and the fate of Jesus are intertwined. The gospel has presented them both as proclaimers of the kingdom of Heaven; it has associated them both with divine wisdom. Now their common fate is recognized: the narrative of the beheading of John points forward to the Trial and Passion of Jesus. Matthew ascribes to Herod the motive of revenge: it was *on account of Herodias* (v.3; the detail about *Herodias* being *his brother Philip's wife* may be incorrect, if the Jewish historian Josephus is to be believed; Philip may have been Herodias' son-in-law, and so married to Salome). In addition to the comment that John had told Herod '*You have no right to her*' (v.4), Matthew also speaks of Herod's desire to kill the Baptist for a different if related reason: *Herod would have liked to put him to death, but he was afraid of the people, in whose eyes John was a prophet* (v.5). Perhaps in this respect Matthew's version of the story is a little closer to the truth than Mark's. Mark simply speaks of Herod's fear of John. The political realities favour Matthew's version. The people would certainly have been on John's side, and when popular support for John became evident that would have required Herod to act. But Herod courted disaster by taking John prisoner; it caused intense hatred from outside and inside his kingdom. Whatever the historical truth of the matter, according to both Matthew and Mark, Herod is the villain. As far as John's death is concerned, the gospel record lays the blame firmly on the king. That is even clearer if v.9 means not just that Herod Antipas was distressed at Herodias' plot and her daughter's complicity, but that

he was completely appalled at the potentially calamitous consequences of his rash promise. In any case here is tyranny painted in
its darkest colours. It is a story which belongs with the slaughter of
the innocents (2.16–18). *Then John's disciples came and took away the
body, and buried it; and they went and told Jesus* (v.12)

C. Feeding and Miracle: the Five Thousand
14.13–21

The following narrative, the Feeding of the Five Thousand, can be
read in many different ways. Jesus' care for the people contrasts
strongly with the villainy of Herod, and even with the unimagina-
tiveness of the disciples. He is concerned for the sick and heals them
(see v.14: *he healed those who were sick*, and compare that with the
parallel verse in Mark 6.34, 'They were like sheep without a
shepherd'). One of the other curious features of Matthew's version
as compared with Mark's is that although the disciples find fish as
well as bread ('*All we have here*', they said '*is five loaves and two fish*':
v.17), when the disciples make the distribution to the men, women
and children, only bread is mentioned (v.19). Some take this to mean
that not only does the death of John point forward to the Passion of
Jesus, the feeding of the multitude does so also. It anticipates Jesus'
final prophetic supper with his friends. There is certainly a dramatic
sub-text beneath the story: the fourfold action 'took, blessed, broke,
gave' (v.19) has parallels throughout the history of the eucharistic
liturgy. The late hour, the place apart, the people arriving on foot,
the compassion and healing, the direction to the disciples (v.16), the
role of the disciples are all additional features by which the story told
would have become part of a cultic act, recalling the commission of
Jesus, demarcating the place and time as holy, and celebrating a
common privilege. As far as the miraculous feeding of the multitude
is concerned, the modern reader finds it difficult to get past the initial
impressions left by this story. It is about actions of Jesus which in
some respects have little parallel in our normal experience (v.20).
Some of the features of the story are entirely familiar. In addition to
its eucharistic features, there is a further well-established pattern.
The movement of the narrative in this chapter has been as follows:
Jesus was searching for some peace after the trauma of John's death
(v.13) ; this is interrupted by the arrival of a crowd; his concern for

them leaves him no option but to provide for their needs. Having provided for their needs he makes a further attempt to secure some peace, and spends the night in prayer – as Matthew twice indicates, *alone* (v.23). He himself fulfils his own pattern of prayer (6.6).

D. *Miracles on Sea and Land*
14.22–36

Matthew's picture of Jesus takes on a new feature: Matthew presents him as a person of decision, who keeps the initiative; but here there is also a divine presence. The firmness by which space for prayer was secured is evident as the disciples are despatched to the other side of the lake (v.22b: *he made the disciples embark*) and the crowds persuaded to break up and go home (v.22c: *he dismissed the crowd*). These decisive actions create the scenario not only for the time of prayer which follows (v.23), but for what is to happen in the next episode: the disciples were *battling with a head wind and a rough sea. Between three and six in the morning he came towards them, walking across the lake* (vv.24f.). Here the story ceases to resemble our normal experience and there are problems in our reading of it. That would not have been true of the first readers. They would have recognized it as a story of divine disclosure. In so far as they knew the Old Testament they would have recognized what Jesus did as a divine activity. It is God who walks on the face of the waters (Job 9.8); he alone strides across the waves of the deep (Psalm 77.19), bringing the powers of chaos under control. When the narrative reaches this point and Jesus approaches his disciples, walking on the water, the first readers would have sensed the majestic claim implicit in the gospel narrative. The one who sent the disciples on ahead of him and strode across the water moved with a divine resourcefulness. The human actors in the drama cry out *in terror: 'It is a ghost!'* (v.26), and their terror enables the true significance of the occasion to be made clear. It is not simply that the situation is within the divine power to control and direct; God's very presence is there: . . . *at once Jesus spoke to them: 'Take heart! It is I; do not be afraid'* (v.27). It is Jesus himself, using the words of divine disclosure (Isaiah 43.1–3). What is disclosed in Jesus is the divine presence, delivering and calming.

We have already noticed the role of the disciples in Matthew. Among the disciples Peter has a distinctive place, often as the one who poses key questions (Matthew 15.15; 18.21) or as the one among the disciples who, as here, takes the initiative. He too is granted, even if fleetingly, a share in that divine power, as he attempts to walk towards Jesus (v.29). A special authority is given to him (16.19; see §9 A), although this appears to be shared with the other disciples in 18.18. Peter also shares with all the disciples a fallibility, an incompleteness of faith. This is represented in several Matthean narratives and dramatically in the story of Peter coming to Jesus on the water. He begins well but then starts to sink and cries out in fear. The fallibility of the disciples, and especially of Peter, is both warning and comfort. The reader is warned against Peter's errors, but encouraged by Peter's periodic acts of faith.

Peter's fear is particularly important. He cries out in terror: '*Save me, Lord!*' (v.30). Fear is a recurrent theme of Matthew's gospel. We have already seen that there is much which might inspire fear. In 13.23 the fear concerns failure to produce fruit; in 25.25 the fear immobilizes the servant and makes him unable to credit his master with kindly motives. Sometimes the fear is justified; it is so in 17.6 where the disciples are terrified by the awesome events of the Transfiguration. The circumstances of Christian living can sometimes provoke a fear. If, as in 14.30, it is a paralysing fear then the reader is made aware that deliverance is possible. Jesus catches hold of Peter and brings him safely to the boat: '*Why did you hesitate?*' he said. '*How little faith you have!*' (v.31). The deliverance is achieved by divine resourcefulness.

The story is a parable of disclosure and of deliverance. It introduces a summary statement of healings (14.34–36) and a series of other stories (chs.15–17) in which our attention is drawn to participants who react to Jesus in various ways. It is not only the parables which encourage us to experiment with fresh responses to the world, to Jesus and to God; these narratives also have a similar function. Like the participants in the parables who engage our interest, our sympathy or our disapproval, the participants in the following chapters do the same. Their story is told simply, in such a way that we find it necessary to fill in details ourselves, so that the story is complete to our satisfaction, and to that extent we become involved in the narrative. The reactions which call us to a deeper faith and commitment are not always those of the disciples, and certainly not only Peter's. There are others models for Christian living in Matthew's gospel. Nevertheless at this stage in the gospel the narratives concerning Peter are particularly interesting, showing how someone with little faith became, in dependence on Christ, a reliable testimony to him; they are signposts on the route of discipleship.

E. *The Pharisees: True and False Speech*
15.1–20

The Pharisees and scribes from Jerusalem question the disciples' daily style of life: '*Why do your disciples break the ancient tradition? They do not wash their hands before eating*' (v.2). Jesus' response is direct and critical: '*Why do you break God's commandment in the interest of your tradition?*' (v.3) This is in some ways a distasteful area of Matthew. Jesus attacks the Pharisees with a disturbing degree of ferocity (15.12–14). There is a real antipathy here toward the Pharisees. They are described as blind guides (15.14; 23.16). They are not the heavenly Father's planting (15.13); they are hypocrites (23.13). The antipathy is not unique to the gospel of Matthew; it is found elsewhere. It is true that sometimes the author of the gospel is held to be responsible for creating this distasteful impression. But a comparison with Mark and Luke suggests otherwise; the Pharisees are treated harshly in Mark and Luke as well (Matthew 12.24 and Mark 3.22; Matthew 23.23–27 and Luke 11.39–44). The condemnation of the Pharisees has a long history and Matthew's gospel is only one stage in that history. But there is also another side to the picture. What Jesus has to say about the Pharisees in Matthew is not all bad. They are even commended on one occasion; and the commendation is genuine: 'The scribes and Pharisees occupy Moses' seat; so be careful to do whatever they tell you' (Matthew 23.2–3a). Moreover distaste at the fierceness of the attack on the Pharisees is reflected in the Matthean text itself. The disciples express it in 15.12: '*Do you know that the Pharisees have taken great offence at what you have been saying?*' What then could have caused so profound a disagreement between Jesus and the Pharisees – a disagreement which, even after the word of caution from the disciples, was repeated ever more forcefully? It is almost impossible to answer that question. We know too little and in insufficient detail about the arguments between Jewish groups at the time of Jesus and at the time of Matthew's writing. We can only guess at who these 'Pharisees' really were and at how representative or unrepresentative they might have been of the teachers of their day. All we can deduce from Matthew 15.4–9 is that for some people ritual dedication of family funds was sufficient excuse for evading family

93

responsibilities, whereas for Jesus that was a superficial response. It was lip-service: *This people pays me lip-service, but their heart is far from me; they worship me in vain, for they teach as doctrines the commandments of men* (vv.8f.). Jesus regards tradition here as tantamount to finding a religious excuse to evade God's demand. It meant turning religion into something external, superficial and ungodly. Little wonder the disagreement was profound – it concerned the nature of true religion. The true nature of religion in terms of Matthew's gospel is down-to-earth service in a world which belongs to God. It is a matter of the words we say and the words we write. The everyday is reviewed in the light of God's presence. Far from being irrelevant to that which is spiritual the everyday is of the very essence of religion. That is the interpretation given to the saying of Jesus: '*No one is defiled by what goes into his mouth; only by what comes out of it*' (15.10). V.10 is treated as a parable (v.15: *Then Peter said, 'Tell us what that parable means'*). The interpretation (vv. 16–20) expands what we read in 12.36. 'every thoughtless word you speak you will have to account for on the day of judgement'. Words are significant because they are a test of personal honour; they reveal what we think and who we are: '*what comes out of the mouth has its origins in the heart; and that is what defiles a person*' (v.18); so they are a test of social honour too; they betray the real state of our spoiled and disfigured relationships (v.19). These are the pointers to true religion. True religion cannot be defined just in terms of ritual actions and prescribed activities (v.20). We are back in the arena of the Sermon on the Mount – required to make responsible decisions in this world as God's world.

F. Faith in the Healer
15.21–28

15.21   *Jesus then withdrew to the region of Tyre and Sidon*, that is, to an area outside Galilee, although Matthew and the Matthean audience may only have been aware of this as another Gentile area. The narrative contains an astonishing conversation. It begins with an appeal from a non-Israelite (Matthew calls her a Canaanite – so an anti-Israelite according the biblical tradition) on behalf of her daughter (v.22). She pleads for a messianic act of healing: '*Son of David! Have pity on me; my daughter is tormented by a devil.*' Jesus does not answer (v.23). To judge by the conversation that follows the disciples are also eager for an act of healing – to get rid of this plague of a woman (v.23)! Jesus reminds them that he is sent only to Israel (v.24; see 10.5). The implication is that healing was an integral part of his ministry, and so healing bears that limitation also. The subsequent exchange between Jesus and the woman cuts to the heart of what the mission of Jesus was about. Religious and racial requirements appear to mean that Jesus cannot help. She is not a Jew; and he is only sent to Jews: he must save the food (exclusively?) for 'the children' (v.26; Mark 7.27 refers to the children as a priority; not so Matthew). *'True, sir'*, *she answered*, but looking after the children does not mean that there will not be scraps left over for the animals from the tables of their master (v.27). Common wisdom provides a critique of religious requirements. Jesus challenged others to meet responsibilities laid upon them by God and to refuse any religious evasion of them. Now, at her prompting, that is the way he acts himself. So in the end the disciples had their wish – but not before the Cannanite woman had been commended for her faith (v.28); and her faith was expressed in a piece of common household wisdom.

G. *Compassion and Feeding: The Four Thousand*
15.29–39

Jesus returns to Galilee (the REB in v.29 gives an over-precise rendering: *Jesus took the road by the sea of Galilee*; the geography of this passage – the route from the North, the sea, the hill – is anything but precise). All that happens – the healing of the lame, the blind, the dumb and the crippled, and the feeding of the large multitude (v.30) – is a repetition of what we read in 4.24, 8.16, 9.35, 14.36. That is our modern Western way of responding: we respond to the text by saying, we have read it all before. The gospel was written out of a context very different from ours. Repetition in that context was not a weakness, a loss of interest, a failure. It had the value of a reminder, a re-enforcement, a recapitulation. It prevented the mind from losing track of the essentials. It helped to give the gospel a clear focus. That does not mean that the repetition is without any variation. On the contrary the very fact of the repetition allows us to savour the differences. Take two examples of these differences: first, the *praise to the God of Israel* (v.31), which is how a Gentile audience would express itself. Then there is the function of the disciples in the feeding narrative: In both 14.19 and 15.36 the disciples are given food by Jesus and told to serve the food to the multitude. But, whereas in 14.14f. it is the disciples who show the initiative by suggesting that it is time for the people to go, in 15.21 it is Jesus who shows the initiative. His concern shows itself in sharing the problem with them: In 14.15 the disciples want to send the crowd off to buy food for themselves; in 15.33 they face the problem which Jesus has posed and despair of finding enough to answer the problem. In these ways the apparent repetitions serve to highlight different relationships between Jesus and the disciples. They are the ones who serve with and on behalf of Jesus. They do so without apparently recollecting what has happened before. Do they perhaps, like the readers, quickly forget what has happened, extraordinary and memorable though it was? A review of ch. 15 can take that reflection a stage further. Around Jesus are different kinds of people responding to him in different ways. The participants in the stories are varied enough to draw us into the narrative and to help us make the story our story. The variations help to secure that involvement. Even the crossing of the lake once more is given a new touch – this time it is to Magdala (where Mary came from, on the western shore), or as Matthew called it using its more traditional name, Magadan (v.39).

H. Testing, Open and Hidden
16.1–12

This is the second of the passages linking the Pharisees with the Sadducees (see 3.7–12 and §2B): *The Pharisees and Sadducees came, and to test him they asked him to show them a sign from heaven* (v.1). The act of requesting a sign is a double problem. They had not used their eyes to see what is happening around them. If they had, they would have begun to repent. In the REB the illustration from weather conditions (16.2f.) is placed in a footnote. But the illustration fits the controversy well: it is specifically about 'the heavens'. The Pharisees and Sadducees know how to use their eyes, as everyone else does, in forecasting weather conditions by looking at the state of the heavens; they may not have seen cosmic signs but they have seen the multitudes fed and healed. Yet they still ask for a sign. The verses are in the footnote because early witnesses to the text of the Matthew omit the passage. That could be because the original of Matthew did not have those verses. Alternatively the original might have used the illustration and a copyist failed to transcribe it because in the copyist's part of the world red sky in the morning did not signify rain. The first problem is then that they fail to use their eyes. But the act of requesting a sign is also a problem because it is hypocritical; they do not really expect a sign. So Jesus offers only a brusque reminder of Jonah (see 12.38; 16.17 and § 6F). That is all he says, and immediately turns away (v.4). They are now presumably on the western shore of Galilee, and when Jesus speaks to the disciples about '*leaven*' (v.6), they assume (vv.5,7) that it is a hidden rebuke for not taking food for the crossing. 'Leaven' can refer to bread making, or to religious impurity, and the conversation rests on the confusion between the two. Jesus was warning his disciples against those who represent a false religion (v.6); they are to beware of leaven in that sense. But the disciples misunderstand his meaning, and take 'leaven' to refer to baked bread (v.7). That misunderstanding reinforces the accusation that there is falseness about their religion: '*Why are you talking about having no bread? Where is your faith?*' (v.8). They have betrayed their anxiety about food, whereas in the feeding of the five thousand and the four thousand food was provided when it was needed and in abundance (vv.9f.). Behind the conversation lie also the mission instructions given in 10.9–11. The disciples are no better than the Pharisees and Sadducees; they have not used their eyes either. The disciples needed to watch out for destructive leaven in themselves: *Then they understood: they were to be on their guard, not against baker's leaven, but against the teaching of the Pharisees and Sadducees* (v.12).

§9 Son of God, Son of Man
16.13–17.27

A. Caesarea Philippi
16.13–28

When he came to the territory of Caesarea Philippi, Jesus asked his disciples, *'Who do people say that the Son of Man is?'* (v.13). Jesus arrives in Caesarea Philippi, a town north of the Sea of Galilee at the foot of Mount Hermon. In Matthew he asks a question about the Son of Man; in Mark the question is phrased differently: 'Who do people say I am?' (Mark 8.27); the reason for the use of Son of Man instead of the first person pronoun 'I' is probably to prepare the way for an explicit linking together in this passage of three terms: 'Son of Man', the suffering humiliated one, coming in judgement yet himself unjustly judged, 'Messiah', the one who fulfils God's promise of restoration, and 'Son of the Living God' (v.16), the agent of God's powerful sovereignty. This explanation fits with the disciples' initial fourfold response in Matthew to Jesus' question (v.14): *'Some say John the Baptist, others Elijah, others Jeremiah, or one of the prophets.'* The initial responses concentrate on the aspect of persecution; all, especially Jeremiah (note that his name is absent from the parallel in Mark 8.28), were persecuted for proclaiming divine judgement ; the first three were also regarded as mystical figures capable of later manifestation on earth. Prompted by Jesus' further question (v.15), Peter adds to the disciples' initial response: *'You are the Messiah, the Son of the living God.'* If Peter's confession of faith here is distinctive (see 14.33), it is in his use of the phrase *living God*. Solemn and evocative, it recalls pictures of redemption (Psalm 41.3 LXX; Revelation 7.2), of holiness (Matthew 26.63), of judgement on arrogance and idolatry (Isaiah 37.4; Acts 14.15; II Corinthians 6.16; I Thessalonians 1.19) and of power over evil and death (see John 1.1–4 and 16.18b). In Matthew's gospel (contrast Mark and Luke) Jesus responds by calling Peter *'Simon, son of Jonah'* (elsewhere he is called 'son of John'), and *'favoured'* because his confession was a revelation from *'my heavenly Father'*. 'Son of Jonah' is a mysterious and subtle reminder of Jonah's gift from God of prophetic insight, a gift linked in the targumic tradition with Deuteronomy 30.11–14, a passage full of insights into the nature of revelation; mysterious, because such a divine empowering is beyond human direction: *'You did not learn that from a human being'* (see Ecclesiasticus 39.6); subtle, because it refers back to 16.4 and forward to the authorization which Peter can now be given (16.18f.). Parallel to Peter's confession of Jesus as the Christ is Jesus' renaming of Simon bar Jonah as Peter (v.18): *'You are Peter, the rock; and on this rock I will build my church, and the powers of death shall never conquer it.'* Peter is his new nickname, although the reason for the nickname is not altogether clear. The play on words has multiple possibilities, and nicknames often mock an opposite characteristic. So what did Jesus mean? 'You are Petros (Peter), and on this *petra* (if *petra* stands for Cephas, on this bed-rock, crag, or boulder) I will build my church . . .': Peter could prove a rock to stumble over (see Matthew's use in 16.23, distinctive among the synoptic parallels, of 'stumbling block' to describe Peter). He could be vacillating and unreliable, the very opposite of a rock. But in 16.18 Peter is the rock on which the new community could be built, as Abraham was described in rabbinic writings as the rock on which God could erect a new world to replace the old (Yalkut I.766 [Numbers 23.9]). The arguments have raged across the centuries over the phrase 'on this rock': does it mean on Peter, or on Peter's confession? But the text is clear: Peter was divinely inspired and this was the reason for his new function and the basis of his authorization. His function was to provide for Jesus Christ the beginnings of a stronghold, a people of God, to stand against all the powers of evil and death (literally 'the gates of Hades' see Isaiah 38.10), parallel to the temple which with its rock resisted the cosmic powers of chaos (Psalms 24 and 46). They are God's people, the church (the *ekklesia*, that is, an assembly standing over against the synagogue and embodying with all other such assemblies the mission of Christ the Lord; see 18.17, the only other use of *ekklesia* in the synoptic gospels, where the – possibly misleading – translation 'congregation' is used); as the church they represent God's sovereign power over evil (18.18b) and rely upon a new kind of divine authorization, different from that of the synagogue or the temple. This authorization is given to Peter; so Peter is not only a stronghold against evil; he also is responsible for giving the community shape and direction. Once again in this passage it is the targumic interpretation of the Old Testament which explains the movement of thought. Isaiah 22.22 reads 'I shall place the key of David's palace on his shoulder; what he opens none will shut, and what he shuts none will open.' Originally this prophesied a replacement of self-seeking Shebna by Eliakim, but it was later interpreted during the long and chequered history of the high-priesthood as the removal of one office-holder by another. So, in Peter's case, rights and privileges pass to him: Jesus said, *I will give you the keys of the kingdom of Heaven*. But what are these rights and privileges and how are they exercised? They are exercised in relation to heaven and earth (16.17,19), and this binds Peter and the church together. The unity of Peter and the church is explained in relation to heaven and earth. Heaven and earth in Matthew are not distinct geographical areas. They are however different realms and relate to different kinds of existence (see § 12 J). Some individuals have access to both. Revelation from heaven brings light into human existence; that is part of the Matthean mysticism. It is the context for the Matthean understanding of Jesus as Son of God: the Son has revealed the wisdom of God and the way of God. So Peter could make his confession only in so far as that confession was revealed to him (16.17), and revealed to him from heaven. But 16.18f. indicate that there are other aspects to this relation of heaven and earth. Responsibility is a trust given from heaven to earth; that also is a feature of Matthean mysticism. We have already recognized this in Matthew 9.8. An authority has been given which extends from the work of Jesus and involves others because of him. In Matthew 16.19 this responsibility includes the making of decisions. Decisions on earth have to be made which have validity in heaven. Precisely what kind of decisions those might be is not stated with any clarity. They may include decisions about the Christian way or about the life of the church. But what is clear is that human responsibility is a gift from heaven; and it is to be used accordingly: *what you forbid on earth shall be forbidden in heaven* (18.19c). Some translators deny that this is what Matthew intended; they translate the passage 'what you forbid on earth will have been forbidden in heaven'; i.e. the decision in heaven comes first; and Peter's decision follows; responsibility consists in following the dictates of heaven. But that interpretation does not fit the parallel passage in 18.18f., where the same phrases are used, and where the request on earth clearly precedes the decision in heaven. As in the case of the classic Old Testament prophets, Peter has to take the responsibility of action and decision, discovering how it relates to the divine will as events unfold. The responsibility involves risk; it is given to Peter on the basis of the divinely-given authority, but the decisions he makes are his decisions, decisions for which he is responsible; and, for that reason if for no other, if he is wise, he will share the task with others (18.18). It is an awesome responsibility; as we have seen, the individual Christian has to take personal responsibiliy for making decisions in living out the way of Jesus; now we see a leader given responsibility in the guiding of the community, for the development and custody of community values. No wonder that it is a responsibility which should be shared.

This raises one of the most fascinating issues regarding Matthew's gospel. If the responsibility of leadership is a shared responsibility, how does that relate to the actual life of the church in and around Antioch? For close to the time when Matthew was written, Antioch had a bishop, Ignatius, who claimed in his letters significant personal authority. The following points need to be made: First, the character of Ignatius' episcopal authority has recently been redefined; a bishop must, according to Ignatius, pray for the invisible things to be revealed to him, and must be 'capable of the mystical vision which can see the incarnated events of salvation history behind the accidental sequences of the present liturgical assembly';[1] such a bishop was the earthly counterpart of the heavenly occupants of the eternal throne, God and the Lamb; in this sense he was 'founded on an immovable rock' (Ignatius, *Letter to Polycarp* 1.1). Second, Matthew's gospel reflects in ch.16 the same mystagogical approach to leadership, i.e. leadership depends on the ability to enter the holy of holies and grasp what flesh and blood could not reveal. Unlike Ignatius, however, Matthew (28.19) laid great stress on the various traditions to be passed on, and therefore also on the historical continuity between what Jesus did and the life of the church. Third, what Matthew says about Peter does not deny the basis of Ignatius' episcopacy, but it qualifies it significantly by the stress on responsibility in the search for and in the attempt to fulfil the Father's will, especially as that responsibility is shared with others and ultimately with all the church (see also 23.8–12). Matthew's gospel emerged from a context of conflicting approaches to leadership, and within that debate the variety and strength of the traditions have an important long-term effect; theyremain today of

[1]A. Brent, *Augustinianum* (Quadrimestre Instituti Patristici), Rome 1987, pp. 347–76.

profound importance in modern ecumenical discussion of the papacy and the historic episcopate.

In Mark's version of the Caesarea Philippi episode Jesus shifts the discussion from himself as Messiah to himself as suffering Son of Man; Peter has proclaimed him as Messiah and this must not be disclosed; instead Jesus gives a threefold prophecy: the Son of Man will suffer and be vindicated. In Matthew Peter proclaims Jesus as Messiah, the Son of the Living God, and as in Mark this messiahship must not be disclosed (v.20). Thus far Mark and Matthew are parallel. But what follows in Matthew does not immediately mention the Son of Man (see 16.21). Matthew uses the same three prophetic pillars of suffering and vindication (Mark 8.31/Matthew 16.21; Mark 9.31/Matthew 17.22; Mark 10.33/Matthew 20.17–20), but they are given a different setting. Perhaps Matthew has already said so much about the revelation of the Son of God that the relationship between messiahship, Son of God and the Son of Man is inevitably different in Matthew from what it is in Mark. The different setting in Matthew includes two particular features: The first is that the argument with Peter is more intense. In Mark's gospel Peter takes exception to what Jesus says about the Son of Man and is rebuked by Jesus with the words 'Out of my sight, Satan!' In Matthew Peter says that what Jesus foretells cannot happen, and the rebuke to Peter is: '*Out of my sight, Satan; you are a stumbling block to me. You think as men think, not as God thinks*' (v.23). The responsibility given to Peter in Matthew is greater than in Mark; and this means that he is exposed to a greater danger. The second feature which distinguishes the Matthean context is this: In Mark the warning to keep silent and the prophecy about the Son of Man lead into a description of discipleship; discipleship involves taking up one's cross; it means shame shared here and glory shared with the Son of Man at his (apparently) imminent coming. In Matthew the sequence is similar: discipleship involves taking up one's cross (v.24); it involves loss here (vv.25f.) and glory shared with the Son of Man (vv.27a, 28: '*there are some of those standing here who will not taste death before they have seen the Son of Man coming in his kingdom*'). But there are three differences: in Matthew there is greater stress on personal, individual responsibility; the reward will be 'to each according to what each does' (v.27c; the force of this is obscured in the REB: *everyone his due reward*); second, the one who gives us responsibility is the Son of Man accompanied by his angels (v.27b); and the final phrase of the chapter refers to the Son of Man's kingdom (as distinct from the parallels in Mark 9.1 and Luke 9.27), offering a possible reinterpretation of the Marcan tradition. Are Peter, James and John (three of those standing there) to glimpse this kingdom momentarily in ch.17?

B. *The Transfiguration*
17.1–8

Six days later (a precise sense cannot be given to the time reference; see Leviticus 23.34 for one possibility) the powerful heavenly Lord is glimpsed by three of the disciples in a transfiguration on the mountain (v.1). The heavenly vision (see v.9) fills them with fear and they see the true nature of the one with whom they live and work. He is the one who will come as judge of all. The vision is described in evocative language. There is the powerful imagery concerning the appearance of Jesus (v.2): *his face shone like the sun, and his clothes became a brilliant white.* That imagery recalls both the tradition of transformation based directly on the story of Moses on Sinai (Exodus 34.35; II Corinthians 3.18) and the language of the open heaven found in Daniel (see Daniel 7.9) and in many Jewish and Jewish Christian writings additional to the Old Testament (e.g. the Testament of Abraham A7, where the key issue is the final judgement on all nations). The experience of the disciples is made more awesome by the presence of Moses and Elijah: *And they saw Moses and Elijah appear, talking with him* (v.3). They are representative figures: Jesus fulfils the law and the prophets; their presence confirms that function and the associated imagery underlines it. But their presence is also symbolic: In both Mark and Matthew, Moses and Elijah point to suffering and vindication; they both suffered in obedience to God's purpose. They were both part of God's purpose for Israel; they suffered and were persecuted because of it. The shelters proposed by Peter for Jesus, Moses and Elijah (v.4) also recall a variety of contexts: bedouin hospitality for honoured guests, the feast of booths (Jubilees 16.26), the tent of meeting (Exodus 33.7–11), and the tabernacling of a heavenly being in human form (Prayer of Joseph A4). So also the *bright cloud* which *suddenly cast its shadow over them* (v.5) recalls the glory of the Lord (Exodus 40.35) and Jeremiah's preparation for the return of the divine glory in the last days (II Maccabees 2.8). The climax of the vision is reached in v.5b: a voice called from the cloud:

'*This is my beloved Son, in whom I take delight; listen to him.*' What was affirmed at his baptism is now reaffirmed at the Transfiguration (17.5), a reaffirmation specifically for the sake of the disciples. The disciples are to listen to him; his words carry divine authority. The heavenly voice (see Genesis 22.11), the terror of the disciples (v.6; see Ezekiel 1.28b), the encouragement given them (v.7; see Daniel 10.12), and the disappearance of Elijah and Moses (v.8) all emphasize the divine authority of Jesus. This provides the clue to the powerful and evocative imagery of the vision: The three disciples witness the eternal validity of what Jesus teaches; what he teaches reflects the eternal sovereignty of the divine will; and the imagery of the transfiguration anticipates both the universal authority of the Risen Christ in 28.18–20 and the vision of final judgement in 25.31–46. Matthew can speak of the Son of Man's kingdom; the Son of Man has a share in the ultimate sovereignty of God and is himself part of the realization of that sovereignty on earth.

C. *John the Baptist and Elijah*
17.9–13

The disciples are commanded not to tell anyone of their vision until after the resurrection (v.9). In the following verses they raise the question of Elijah's role (v.10): '*Why then do the scribes say that Elijah must come first?*' Precisely why they do so and why they do so in that form is not clear. Presumably the appearance of Elijah as part of the vision might have been supposed to be the trigger. But the form of the question seems to require a further explanation. Is it that the command to silence appears to contradict the scribal theory of a public appearance of Elijah preparing for the Messiah, or taking up his work of waking the dead? Elijah the prophet is a testimony to Jesus' fulfilment of the work of all the prophets; he is also the one who was expected to inaugurate that fulfilment: '*Elijah is to come and set everything right*' (v.11); but such a public restoration makes the command to silence seem pointless. Matthew's version of Jesus' response in v.12 suggests that there had been just such an appearance, but the scribes failed to recognize him (v.12). Instead they acted in his case just as they pleased, as they will in Jesus' case also. What Jesus had hinted at in his command to silence, had indeed already been anticipated, in the Baptist's death: '*in the same way the*

Son of Man is to suffer at their hands.' The disciples then realize (v.13) that in a sense Elijah had come; the fulfilment had been inaugurated. Their own eyes had witnessed it; it was John the Baptist, the one who had suffered and been persecuted for proclaiming repentance, and who had said: The kingdom of Heaven is upon you! The perspective of John the Baptist as preparing the way, as living out gospel values, as an expression of the divine wisdom, and like wisdom ignored and rejected, gives the Transfiguration a historical thrust. The vision of Elijah alongside the heavenly Lord of glory has an humble counterpart in the Baptist's work, in his challenge to righteousness, his proclamation of the kingdom and his death in its cause. The fulfilment has been inaugurated and so the command to silence will hold until the fulfilment is complete.

D. A Cure: Failure and Faith
17.14–21

In comparison with the Marcan story of the Epileptic Boy the Matthean is brief. It is as if the contrast between the glory of the disciples' experience and the bathos of their inability to help needs no elaboration. The contrast is made simply, with a minimum of detail. It is the familiar picture of a descent from the mountain-top experience to the realities of the valley below: *When they returned to the crowd* . . . (v.14). They have witnessed the power of the Lord; but when a father brings his epileptic son to them they remain fallible and helpless: the father complains to Jesus *'I brought him to your disciples, but they could not cure him'* (v.16). However the brevity of the Matthean story gives it a further dimension. It brings into close proximity the disciples' failure and Christ's authority: *Then Jesus spoke sternly to him; the demon left the boy, and from that moment he was cured* (v.18). Such a stark contrast might strike the reader today as unhelpful, as indeed the association between epilepsy and demon-possession would seem misguided. If repeated again and again, an emphasis on the authority of Jesus might suggest that we are left with nothing that we can do. But in this story Matthew has something else in mind. His shorter version serves to highlight a balancing feature: the tension between the disciples' inadequate faith (v.17 *'What an unbelieving and perverse generation!'*) and the power of faith, even faith no bigger than a mustard seed (v.20): *'if you have faith no bigger than a mustard seed, you will say to this mountain, 'Move from here to there!' and it will move.'* In his version of the story Mark is concerned to stress the importance of prayer (Mark 9.29), and there are many passages where that can be said of Matthew. Indeed some early manuscripts of Matthew include Mark 9.29 as v.21 (see the REB margin). Prayer is the means by which the disciple receives strength; in order to match the demands of the disciples' vocation, it is essential that they have time alone with God. Both Mark and Matthew agree on that. But Matthew seems to provide the reader with a further key to the healing narratives. It is not so much that we are fallible and Jesus is the great healer; it is more that the great healer never departs from our company. He continues with us and amongst us. Seen from the point of the Matthean gospel as a whole he continues with us sometimes as one with the healer, sometimes as one with the sufferer. So even the beginnings of faith can see the enormous possibilities (v.20). Because of God's active presence, *nothing will be impossible for you* (see 19.26); for the healer and for the sufferer, there is hope. The believer 'laughs at impossibilities and cries "It shall be done!" ' (*Hymns and Psalms* 693).

E. The Son of Man: Death and Resurrection
   17.22f.

17.22   *They were going about together in Galilee . . .* The setting for the second declaration of the passion and resurrection is Galilee. Many theories have been built upon this verse, notably that this represents a decisive moment in the gospel narrative, as the disciples gather together to conclude the mission to Israel and begin the universal mission to all peoples. However, as the early translations of the verse show, this is to strain the text beyond what it can bear. It is capable of various translations: they were gathering about him; they were moving around with him; they were conversing with him. That this was a general activity and that it took place in Galilee corresponds with the parallel in Mark 9.30. The force of the paragraph is twofold: first, through repetition of the prophecy: *The Son of Man is to be handed over into the power of men, and they will kill him; then on the third day he will be raised again* (vv.22f.); and second, through the final word of the paragraph: *grief*. The reaction of grief might be considered an advance on Peter's response in 16.22. But if it is an advance, it was short-lived. See the third declaration in 20.17–19.

F. The Temple Tax and Freedom
17.24–27

The Coin in the Fish's Mouth is another story in which Peter figures conspicuously. He is questioned about Jesus' attitude to the temple tax: *'Does your master not pay temple tax?'* The half-shekel mentioned in this passage was a payment due from each Israelite according to Exodus 30.13–15. There was considerable debate as to whether or not the payment of this could be required of all Jews. That it should be required was supported by Pharisees but it was objected to by others. We have evidence of this kind of objection from the Dead Sea Scrolls. It would seem that Jesus here is siding with the latter; he was willing to pay the half-shekel on a single occasion without accepting liability for its regular payment. It is strange to find the story here, since the gospel of Matthew belongs to a period long after the fall of Jerusalem, while the story concerns an issue which belonged specifically to a time when the temple was still standing. It is true that after the fall of Jerusalem Roman authorities replaced the temple tax with a substitute tax which the emperor used to support the temple of Jupiter Capitolinus in Rome. But 17.24–27 makes the best sense when it is understood against the earlier background. According to the narrative Jesus takes up the matter with Peter: *'Tell me, Simon, from whom do earthly monarchs collect tribute money? From their own people, or from aliens?' 'From aliens'*, said Peter. Jesus then appears to claim for himself and his followers freedom from external authorities, the freedom in fact claimed by all who are Jews: *'Yes'*, said Jesus, *'and their own people are exempt'* (v.26). Against the earlier background *their own people* means 'the Jews'; Jews are free to pay or not to pay as they resolve.

This is the first time in the gospel that the theme of freedom has been explicitly stated and it is interesting that it appears in the context of Jewish practice. Fulfilment of this particular requirement of Jewish law was a matter for personal conscience and personal decision. Although it is explicitly stated only here, the concept of freedom stands behind much of what we have read so far. The concept of responsibility has been used freely, and responsibility and freedom go together. The one makes little sense without the other. Responsibility implies that we are free to consider the possible patterns of Christian obedience and to act in accordance with the decisions we make. That was one of the findings of the earlier study on the Sermon on the Mount. So here, freedom includes a freedom to pay the half-shekel tax. That is how the narrative ends. Peter is told to go and catch the fish with the coin in its mouth (v.27). Providing that the payment is not imposed and providing that a single payment is not understood as acceptance of the tax in principle, there is no reason why the miraculous coin should not be paid on behalf of both of them. Their freedom is not thereby infringed; rather it is enhanced by the free decision on that one occasion to pay. Freedom in the New Testament has these important elements: it goes side by side with responsibility; it includes the freedom to decide, and that may be exercised in obedience as well as in resistance (v.27): '. . . *we do not want to cause offence.*' We may choose not to cause offence, as on that occasion Jesus did.

§10 Life in the Kingdom (Discourse 4)
18.1–35

A. Who is the Greatest?
18.1–5

This is the fourth of the five great discourses. It begins with a question and much of the chapter provides various aspects of the answer. *At that time the disciples came to Jesus and asked, 'Who is the greatest in the kingdom of Heaven?'* (v.1). One answer is given as an immediate response: Jesus sets a child in the middle of the disciples: *'unless you turn round and become like children, you will never enter the kingdom of Heaven'* (v.3). This is further explained in vv.4f.: *'Whoever humbles himself and becomes like this child will be the greatest in the kingdom of Heaven, and whoever receives one such child in my name receives me.'* The openness of a child to divine revelation was often recognized by Jewish divines. The biblical pattern is provided by Samuel (I Samuel 3); Samuel's elders were able only to advise; he alone heard the call of God. Humility then means the willingness to live in the world as God's world and to be open to the divine revelation by whatever means it may come. It is also about vulnerability, helplessness and weakness, for it is with these that Jesus identifies himself. That is what greatness is about if we judge by the values of the kingdom. It is not about status, power or authority; but about the aptitude and attitude of the learner, and the preference given to the weak. V.5 adds a further point; a child becomes Christ to the welcoming host. What this means has been presented in many different ways. Perhaps the best way is to approach the passage through the many other contexts in which Christ is spoken of as present – he is present in his disciples, in his little ones, in his community, among those who study his teaching. A child is special in being a symbol of all who need care, attention and protection, who are vulnerable and defenceless, and in whom Christ is present. In Matthew's gospel there is a one to one relationship between such a person and Christ himself. In serving such a one we serve Christ ('anything you did for one of my brothers here, however insignificant, you did for me' 25.40). Sometimes scholars have argued that such a claim could only be made if the child represents a Christian missionary or a Christian church member; 18.1–5 does not mention that kind of qualification and the presentation of a child as an acted parable displacing the disciples as a model argues against such limitations (see also 19.14 and its context; and 18.20 and the notes there). Matthew is not alone in citing a child as suited to the kingdom. In John's gospel Nicodemus is told that he must be born 'again' or 'from above' if he is to enter to kingdom. The helpless potential of a little child carries hopes beyond our adult dreams.

B.   The Little Ones and Responsibility
18.6–10

To this general approach there is however in v.6 an important qualification: the *little ones who believe in me* can be given offence. A recurrent motif in this section of ch. 18 is that of 'offence'. Translators have difficulty here because the Greek word used and from which our word 'scandal' derives is capable of so many variant translations. We have already met it in Jesus' rejoinder to Peter: 'You are an offence (or a stumbling block) to me' (16.23). It can refer to anything which trips us up. In Matthew 18.6–9 some translators take it in a spiritual sense: 'cause to sin' or 'cause to lose faith in me'. This follows from the definition of the little ones as 'those who believe in me'. Other translators prefer a more general translation such as 'be a hindrance to', as in the REB ' cause the *downfall* of'; they consider it possible that the passage can have a wider sense: prevent the development of, offer a bad example to, put temptation in the way of. Those who cause such offence are given stern advice, advice which also appeared in the Sermon on the Mount. Right decisions are so important that the best way to grasp their importance is through overstatement: if you cannot control your hand or foot, go and amputate yourself! (v.8). That is the level of importance which the teacher must attach to work with the vulnerable: '*it is better to enter into life with one eye than to keep both eyes and be thrown into the fires of hell*' (v.9). 18.10 adds a further reason for caring for the 'little ones': '*they have their angels in heaven, who look continually on the face of my heavenly Father.'* No one is quite sure what is meant by the verse. It could mean that the 'real selves' of these little ones are close to God; or the angels could be guardian angels, keeping personal watch over each individual from birth to grave; or these are angels of the divine presence whose care for the 'little ones' ensures God's close acquaintance with their fate. Whichever of these is correct, the point is that offence caused to little ones is all the more serious because of the value placed upon them in the heavenly realm. Perhaps the strongest argument for the last alternative, 'the angels of the presence' is that chapter 18 ends with a story where those who have access to 'the king's ear' relate to him the offence done to one of his servants. Those servants perform on earth the task which the angels perform in heaven.

C. *The Sheep*
18.12–14

The parable of the Sheep ends in Matthew with a reference to the Father's will: *'It is not your heavenly Father's will that one of these little ones should be lost'* (v.14). This makes the parable a conclusion to the first half of the discourse. The first half is concerned with God's little ones, with their place in the kingdom and with the perils attending those who might cause them harm. So God's purpose in caring for them and protecting them is confirmed. The little ones are undefined at the beginning of the chapter; from 18.6 onward they can be understood in the more limited sense as Christian believers. Why they are called 'little ones' is not clear; it could be because they are young, or young in the faith, or simply because they are vulnerable or live in a situation which makes them vulnerable or have strayed into places which makes them vulnerable, perhaps into an environment which they cannot handle. This must often have happened to young Christians in the period between the Jewish War and the writing of Matthew's gospel. Three times Matthew's version of the parable uses the verb *'stray'*: *'suppose. . one of them strays'*, *'the one that strayed'* (v.12), *'delighted over that sheep rather than over the ninety-nine that did not stray'* (v.13). The Matthean parable is therefore more about a wandering sheep than a lost sheep. The concern is for little ones which are vulnerable because they have strayed into dangerous places or even been led astray into them. What is meant by this is suggested in Matthew's text by the associations of the 'scandal' language in the earlier part of the chapter and by the warnings at the beginning of ch.13: worldly cares, the glamour of wealth and the excesses of the flesh lead the Christian astray. There are two facets to the return of the straying sheep. The first is, as in the Lucan parallel, joy over the discovery of the stray. Several of the parables in Matthew emphasize this theme. Matthew's gospel is not only about judgement; it is also about the joy of the kingdom. Faithful servants are told: 'Enter into your lord's joy'. The second facet is, again as in Luke, the contrast between the one and the ninety-nine, with the emphasis on the finding of the one. This coincides with the interest in the individual in the opening section of this chapter, and in the possibility of repentance declared in 13.15.

D. If Someone Does Wrong
18.15–17

The second half of the chapter begins with an example of someone going astray. It is the specific case of a sinful act: *if your brother does wrong* (v.15). Jewish traditions concerning how to deal with such a situation have a long history. It goes back to Leviticus 19.17f. That Leviticus passage says (in summary) four things: reprove the sinner; anger is dangerous; guilt is contagious; the motivation should be love. To follow all four suggestions is quite a feat. Few people can manage it. So in the course of Jewish history the tradition suggested various stages: for example, reprove the sinner person to person (see v.15: *go and take the matter up with him, strictly between yourselves*), but try to make it up before the sun goes down; if that proves unworkable or ineffective then try giving the matter an airing before a larger group (see v.16: *if he will not listen, take one or two others with you*). What is presented here in Matthew is a threefold pattern: person to person, before two or three witnesses, before the church as a whole (*if he refuses to listen to them, report the matter to the congregation*, v.17). What happens if the sinner, after being reproved in all the three ways, still refuses to listen? There is a danger of contagion; and there is the problem of intransigence. The sinner endangers the life of the community, and fails to see the necessity of putting the matter right. An ultimate act of discipline is then essential. It is necessary to treat the sinner *as you would a pagan or a tax-collector* (v.17b). The language has the ring of Jewish discipline about it. It involves exclusion from the community. But is the exclusion to be permanent? Perhaps in

112

some communities it was. Paul did not think of it as an irrevocable act; for Paul the final level of discipline was exclusion from the community, but it was aimed at ultimate restoration. In I Corinthians 5.5 he talks about consigning someone to Satan, with the hope that ultimate salvation may result. In Matthew 18 the aim of exclusion is not made clear. Nor is it easy to reconcile ch. 18 with the policy of 'letting both grow together until the harvest' in 13.30. Nor is it clear whether this was a tradition of discipline which had been handed down and might need contemporary adjustment and modification. But what is clear is that the remainder of Matthew 18 concerns forgiveness. According to this second half of the chapter forgiveness has no limits, unless it is a limit which the sinner imposes. In the latter case forgiveness could be offered again and again and refusal to be forgiven could mean exclusion and ultimate disaster. There seems to be no way back from a self-imposed hell.

E. Two Declarations
18.18–20

In Matthew 16 Peter was given the responsibility of binding and loosing. The task included making decisions about the Christian way or making decisions about the Christian community. In Matthew 18 the responsibility is explicitly a shared one. 'Whatever you bind' has a plural reference: *'whatever you forbid on earth shall be forbidden in heaven, and whatever you allow on earth shall be allowed in heaven.'* It means that all the disciples share the binding and the loosing. Furthermore, the context of Matthew 18 is more specific than in Matthew 16; in Matthew 18 it concerns, as we have seen, forgiveness. Peter asks Jesus how often he is to forgive his brother. This sounds similar to John 20.22f. There the Holy Spirit is breathed on the disciples and they are given new powers; the powers sound similar to those in Matthew 18.18, but in John 20.23 instead of the verbs 'binding' and 'loosing' there are more specific verbs: 'forgiving' and 'retaining'. So the parallel in John 20.23 along with the context in Matthew 18 suggest that 'binding' and 'loosing' in Matthew 18.18 might mean 'declaring forgiven' and 'declaring unforgiven'. In Matthew 16 what is done in heaven and what is done on earth affect each other. What is bound in heaven is bound on earth. That is true also in Matthew 18.19; actions in heaven and actions on earth are related. There is however a difference; in Matthew 18 the promise is given that requests made on earth by the agreement of two will be honoured in heaven. Presumably this means that the request that God would forgive made by two in agreement with each other would be honoured by our heavenly Father. The grounds for this honouring of a request on earth are stated in Matthew 18.20. It is because where two or three are gathered for Christ's sake, he is there in the midst. REB translates the verse: *'For where two or three meet together in my name, I am there among them.'* 'I am there' has a divine ring to it; it recalls the mention of God's presence in 1.23 and it anticipates the promise in 28.20: 'I will be with you to the end of time.' It also recalls the rabbinic saying 'when ten sit together and are occupied with Torah the Shechinah rests among them, as it is said "God stands in the congregation of judges"' (Mishnah, Pirke Aboth 3.6, which suggests also that the number 'ten' could be reduced to a single individual). So Christ's presence means that the agreement on earth has already the divine sanction. The rabbinic parallel raises some important issues about Matthew 18.20: should the phrase 'in my name' be better translated 'for my sake', and is there behind 18.20, as in the rabbinic parallels, a cosmic, mystical sense of the human personality? If the human being is understood in a mystic way in 18.20, as able to mediate the divine presence, could that be true of 18.5,10 and 13 also?

F. On Forgiveness (the Unforgiving Servant)
18.21–35

Peter asks: *'Lord, how often am I to forgive my brother if he goes on wronging me? As many as seven times?'* Jesus' reply suggests that forgiveness could be unlimited. The parable of the Unmerciful Servant follows. As the story begins it sounds as if the parable is about that unlimited character of forgiveness. The lord hears his servant's plea and releases him from an enormous debt. The second part however depicts the servant well-nigh throttling a fellow servant, deaf to his entreaties, and demanding on pain of imprisonment that he should settle a paltry debt. The parable has become a story not about a release from an enormous debt, but about a servant released from an enormous debt who refuses to show mercy to a colleague. So far the parable has been told in an epic style with brief, succinct phrases. There is a final twist to the tale and the final part of the parable where this occurs abounds with Matthean cross-references, as if the epic style had been deliberately expanded. His colleagues report the matter to the lord, who revokes his act of mercy, requiring that the servant be tortured until the debt is paid in full. It has become a story of judgement on an unmerciful servant. The unmerciful servant will find that no mercy will shown to him. The end of the chapter offers a comment on the parable. God will respond as the lord did, if we do not show mercy to others. Those who are forgiven must discover the way to forgive. The end of the chapter takes us still deeper: '*That is how my heavenly Father will deal with you, unless you each forgive your brother from your hearts*' (v.35). It is not only a matter of forgiving because we have been forgiven; we are told to forgive from the heart. That is a startlingly difficult requirement. Like the Israelite in Leviticus called on to reprove a sinner but told that he must reprove without anger and love his neighbour as himself, we are asked to show mercy from the heart. Our motives are under scrutiny. Forgiveness has to come from the heart, and that is impossible unless we discover how we may truly love our neighbour. Matching the intensity of the requirement 'forgive from the heart' is the intensity of the Father's response, 'that is how my heavenly Father will deal with you'. The stories in Matthew often appear to be direct and simple. The more carefully we read them the more searching we find them. Like the Sermon on the Mount they require of us responsible decisions and fresh attitudes, and promise that those attitudes and decisions are of unimaginable significance. They are genuinely matters of life and death.

§11 Questions in Judaea
19.1–20.34

A. About Marriage
19.1–12

Matthew now concludes the discourse with a typical summary and reverts to the Marcan order of events. Jesus arrives in Judaea (v.1; see Mark 10.1): *When Jesus had finished this discourse he left Galilee and came into the region of Judaea on the other side of the Jordan.* The geography in Mark's parallel account is hard to understand, but at least there Judaea and 'beyond the Jordan' are separate phrases. In Matthew they form, as the REB correctly translates it, a single phrase: Judaea is described as being on the other side of the Jordan. Coming from Galilee and crossing the Jordan one would expect to arrive in Peraea, not Judaea. So how is this geographical oddity to be explained? Is Matthew's geography faulty? Is he describing a route to Judaea? Or is Matthew describing Judaea as anyone would who approached Judaea via Damascus taking the eastern route from Antioch or Damascus to the Jordan valley? If the third suggestion is correct, 'on the other side of the Jordan' would refer to the west bank: Jesus came into the region of Judaea on the west bank of the Jordan. There is a difference between Matthew and Mark also in their emphases on what Jesus does in Judaea. Mark emphasizes the teaching work; Matthew says: *Great crowds followed him, and he healed them there* (v.2). Nevertheless three major areas of teaching follow in Matthew: on marriage, on children and on wealth. On marriage Jesus had already in 5.32 restricted the right of divorce to cases involving a serious sexual misdemeanour; he sought security for women within the married state, and he invited mutual responsibility in the relationships between husband and wife. 5.32 came from a tradition shared with Luke. Now Matthew introduces Marcan material on the same subject. Here in ch.19 the Pharisees raise once again the question of how wide the right to divorce might be: '*Is it lawful for a man to divorce his wife for any cause he pleases?'* (v.3). Once again the issue is that of interpretation: how is Deuteronomy 24.1 to be reinterpreted? Instead of giving a direct answer Jesus offers a significant additional emphasis: He grounds marriage, as many of his contemporaries did, in the will of the Creator (v.4): *'Have you never read that in the beginning the Creator made them male and female?'* The principle set out in Genesis 1.26, and the divine act of creating woman from the man (Genesis 2.23), provide from the very beginning the reason why a man leaves his own family, is united with his wife and the two become one flesh (v.5). The consequence is that a husband cannot undo what God has done (v.6). The Pharisees reply that this emphasis, useful though it may be, leaves unexplained Moses' legislation on the matter (v.7). Jesus gives a subtle nuance to his reply which avoids the suggestion that the Mosaic law might be invalid: it was not legislation so much as permission that Moses gave (v.8). The creative purpose of God is prior in every sense to the permission or concession offered by Moses: *'It was because of your stubbornness that Moses gave you permission to divorce your wives; but it was not like that at the beginning'* (v.8). Stubbornness refers to hardness of heart, to human weakness in being unable or unwilling to live in God's world, fulfilling his purposes. The concession was made as an adaptation to human failure. V.9 includes only part of the Marcan material. Mark's material includes a private conversation with the disciples which moves from the question of divorce to the question of remarriage, and deals with divorce initiated by the wife in addition to divorce initiated by the husband. Matthew makes specific provision for divorce, using a similar phrase to that found 5.32, but says nothing here about a divorce which a woman might initiate: *'. . . if a man divorces his wife for any cause other than unchastity, and marries another, he commit adultery.'* The word translated here 'unchastity' could have a very narrow or a very wide meaning: it could mean incest, adultery, pre-marital unchastity or other cases of 'sexual sin'. But whether or not it has the wider sense in this verse, the significance of Jesus' comment would seem to be that while the purpose of God for humanity is clear, inability to live with God's purpose does make concessions necessary, and one of those concessions relates to sexual misbehaviour. The early church can be seen within the New Testament wrestling with the issues of separation and divorce, and introducing other kinds of concessions, for example on the grounds of pastoral considerations such as those of mixed marriages (see I Corinthians 7.12–16). But there is no attempt in Matthew to limit

117

what is said here about marriage and divorce to one particular group or another. The ultimate sanctity of marriage and the pastoral concessions which are essential in daily life are retained by Matthew in a public section of teaching.

The verses which follow are different; they are unique to Matthew and are addressed specifically to the disciples, dealing with a related subject, celibacy. The disciples draw a pessimistic conclusion from what Jesus has said: *'If that is how things stand for a man with a wife, it is better not to marry'* (v.10). But Jesus has established that marriage is part of the original purpose of God for humanity and has grounded marriage in the will of the Creator. So the renunciation of marriage has to be a special gift (v.11). V.11 can mean either that not everyone can understand what Jesus has said or, as REB translates it, *'That is a course not everyone can accept.'* The remainder of the sentence adds to the text an important assumption about the divine will: *'but only those* (can accept it) *for whom God has appointed it.'* There are two ways in which the remainder of the passage can be understood: either (following the REB) that God appoints some to celibacy for the sake of the kingdom, as against those who are celibate by nature or choice (*'For while some are incapable.. there are others who have renounced marriage'*); or that there are given circumstances which mean that certain people do not marry – birth, predilection, vocation – and in all those very different cases celibacy is perfectly acceptable. We prefer the second of these. First, the notion of 'God appointing people' to celibacy is not explicitly part of the text, and in either of the interpretations given above 'gift' (see I Corinthians 7; the Greek phrase means 'to whom it has been given') is more acceptable than 'appointment'. Appointment carries with it the implication of predestination, and, particularly in the second interpretation, predestination to celibacy would reflect unfavourably on the nature of God, and indeed in the case of self-imposed celibacy would appear nonsensical. Second, there is no reason why Matthew should pass over those described in v.12a and 12b as relatively unimportant. Of course we may properly ask who they were. The phrase translated in the REB 'incapable of marriage' would usually be understood as 'incapable of effective sexual activity' (a very literal translation would be 'eunuchs'). Certainly some Christians in the early days of the church did not ostracize eunuchs (Acts 8.27), and there is no reason why Matthew should have marginalized them (see Isaiah 56.3–8 and §12 B). There is of course a serious objection to a literal understanding of 'eunuchs' in v.12: according to a literal understanding of v.12c some

118

early Christians must have emasculated themselves for the sake of the kingdom. While some did this in the service of pagan cults, we have no evidence of the Christian practice as early as Matthew's gospel . But the verse need not be taken literally. It could be another example of exaggeration for emphasis. If it is not exaggeration then v.12c would have to refer either to celibacy (*'others who have renounced marriage'*), or sexual abstinence. Even if we take that view and we decide that those described in v.12 are celibate rather than physically impaired, there is no hint of Matthean scorn; the three circumstances are regarded as parallel. Of the two interpretations the second is preferable. But neither of course is there any hint in the conclusion of Matthean approbation: *'Let those accept who can.'* Marriage remains the key model.

If that is what 19.1–12 meant in its original setting, contemporary discussion of it may need to begin from a quite different standpoint: we should want to begin from the significance before God of the individual as a social being. Only from that standpoint can 'single-ness' be afforded the value which those who are single claim as their right. For fear lest they denigrate the single state, we need to distance ourselves from the some of the biblical assumptions about family and marriage.

B. *The Blessing of the Children*
19.13–15

Once again children are given a central place in the narrative: *They brought children for him to lay his hands on them with prayer*. The laying on of hands with prayer was used in various contexts (as in Acts 8.17). Here what the unspecified adults requested is, first, a symbolic confirmation for the individual child of divine care for every human being and of the covenant love of God for all Israel. It shares this feature with Genesis 48.14 (see 48.15–16a), but lacks of course the specific promise of 48.16c. The specific character of Jesus' action would also have been his promise of the kingdom, its hope and joy.

When the disciples remonstrate with the adults (v.14), Jesus' response is: *'do not try to stop them.'* This is often linked with a feature of early baptismal practice found in Acts 8.36; 10.47; 11.17; but the REB translations of those Acts passages show how differently the verb is being used in each of those cases. It is unlikely that Matthew

19.13–15 had baptismal associations; the Matthean understanding of baptism is represented in 28.19–20. The reason for Jesus' response is given in terms reminiscent of 18.3. Once again the disciples have to give way as children become inheritors of the kingdom.

C. *About the Way of Life*
19.16–22

The third area of teaching in this section is about wealth. A rich young ruler discovers that the demands of the kingdom are way beyond what he anticipates. That is probably the heart of the Matthean version of this conversation. One way of understanding what passes between the rich young man and Jesus is as follows: the young man wants to know how to gain entrance to the kingdom (*'What good must I do to gain eternal life?'* Jesus suggests that this is to oversimplify matters. There is all manner of good that might be required of him (*'Good? . . . Why do you ask me about that?'*); for there is a source initiating all that is good; God *alone . . .* and he *. . . is good*. Nevertheless if the questioner keeps the commandments he will find that an excellent place to begin. *'Which commandments?'* he asks. Only five of the commandments are listed; they are in an interesting order (contrast Deuteronomy 5.17–20) and they are introduced in a way which is not easy to translate. The original text suggests that this selection represents a well-known unit of teaching (v.18): You know the outline – *Do not murder; do not commit adultery; do not steal; do not give false evidence; honour your father and mother*. To these Matthew (although not Mark or Luke) adds as a summary, Leviticus 19.18 : *'love your neighbour as yourself.'* The young man claims to have made an excellent start. 'What do I still lack?' he asks. But the range of good required of him, especially in the use of his possessions, is a different issue. *'If you wish to be perfect'*, says Jesus, *'go, sell your possessions, and give to the poor. .'* The word 'perfect' (see the note on 5.48) indicates a singleness of intention and selflessness of attitude directing and purifying action. That is the kind of demand which discipleship makes. The invitation to follow Jesus on those terms is too much for the young man (v.22). He cannot live up to those kinds of demands. His *great wealth* stands in the way.

D. About Wealth
19.23–26

There is in fact only one way into the kingdom. It is the way which God makes possible. So the rich, who are used to buying their privileges, find entry into the kingdom particularly difficult (v.24): ' *it is easier for a camel to pass through the eye of a needle.'* The absurdity of the picture makes the difficulty obvious to all. There is the temptation to self-reliance, and the assumption that wealth is a divine blessing (Proverbs 10.6; but see Ecclesiasticus 5.1; Matthew has some interesting reflections to make on this matter; see 25.15 and §13 I). This latter assumption could provide the link with the disciples' exclamation: *'Then who can be saved?'* (v.25). Reliance on divine grace is the only way (v.26), says Jesus. But it is a way which is open: *'Everything is possible for God.'* The story of the rich young ruler and the sayings about entry into the kingdom each contribute a part to a much larger picture. The rich young ruler discovered the range of goodness required of him; but that is only a beginning and in no way implied a gaining of the kingdom by merit. For the sayings about the kingdom stress dependence on God. The issues of wealth and the proper use of wealth will dominate some later sections of the gospel. In that way the picture will gradually become complete.

E. About Discipleship
19.27–30

One part of the picture concerns how disciples will fare: *'We have left everything to follow you'* says Peter (v.27). The promise which Jesus gives to them concerns the time of the Son of Man's enthronement (an extremely unusual phrase which is translated in the REB in *the world that is to be*, v.28). They will share that vindication with him; and it will involve a restoration of Israel (the twelve tribes), with the disciples as those who give judgement. They are to share in the fulfilment of all God's promises to and for Israel and they will enjoy recompense for all the sacrifices they have made (v.29). Above all, eternal life will be their inheritance. In Matthew's communities the name Israel would have carried many meanings, some literal and some metaphorical; in that new era of relationships between Israel and the church, the promises of Jesus would have been restated for both Israel and the church, and the metaphors for vindication would have been reminted. What is startling however is the final sentence: *But many who are first will be last, and the last first* (v.30). It is repeated again in v.16 and is a clear warning not to take anything for granted. In context of this chapter it warns that the kingdom of Heaven belongs to children, and in the next chapters it warns that some who expect prominence may be disappointed, and some who anticipated a place in the kingdom will be rejected.

F. *The Workers in the Vineyard*
20.1–16

The parable of the Workers in the Vineyard (20.1–16) also concerns money. The landowner in this parable gives a day's wages to all who on that particular day have worked for him in his vineyard. They all receive the same, irrespective of the number of hours they have worked. They are also paid in the order everyone least expected; it is a case of 'last come, first served' (v.8). The landowner regards this as 'generosity', and whatever we may think of him it might well have appeared so to an ancient economist. Anything less for the labourers enrolled late on in the day would hardly have been worth their while. The ancient economist would have regarded everything as done properly. The landowner pays them all on the spot, including those with whom he agreed a contract. It is the order that is unexpected; the first are last and the last first. The parable repeats what the previous chapter hinted about God: God makes the unexpected possible; he chooses the last to be first. The inclusion in the story of the disgruntled workers is hardly accidental (v.11). If the story is about unexpected generosity, then it will also be about observant eyes. Generosity is greeted by different reactions, and jealousy is often one of them. That is the case here. It used to be thought that parables should have only a single point of interest. But Matthew's parables can rarely be reduced to just one focus, particularly those which are extended epic in style; they seem to be deliberately expanded to give them a wide range of reference. They reflect typical situations in ordinary life, and ordinary life is full of varying reactions and troubled relationships. We found the same in the parable of the Unforgiving Servant. There the colleagues of the unforgiving servant reacted unfavourably to his behaviour. Here the disgruntled workers react unfavourably to their employer. They are like people who see the gracious goodness of God expended on the undeserving and feel that this is all wrong. As Jesus reminded other listeners: God causes the sun to rise on good and bad alike and sends the rain on the just and the unjust. There is a freedom about the activity of God which defies human calculations, and, predictably, human reactions to God can be confused and irritated. New styles of reactions need to be developed, matching instead of resenting the divine graciousness. That is a difficult enough lesson for individuals to learn; it is harder still when racial and religious groups are involved. Features of the parable would have recalled the contrast between the ancient people of God with its centuries of service and the new people of God, some of whom had served the briefest of apprenticeships. It had to be an unusually powerful story for the appeal in those circumstances for new styles of reaction to be successful.

G. *The Son of Man: Death and Resurrection*
20.17–19

Now the destination of Jesus is specifically stated to be Jerusalem: *Jesus was journeying toward Jerusalem* (v.17), and Jesus informs the twelve disciples privately, *on the way* (a typical reference to the Christian pilgrimage), that this is their goal (v.18). For a third time he tells them about his fate. He is to be crucified at the hands of Gentiles (v.19). Matthew alone indicates that his fate is to be crucifixion. The increase in detail (although Matthew omits Mark's reference to spitting) heightens the fearful expectation and is evocative of persecution and martyrdom: *mocked, flogged and crucified* (v.19). As before, what follows the prophecy of the passion is a prophecy that God will raise Jesus from the dead *on the third day* (as in 16.21 and 17.23; in each passage Mark has 'three days after'). So *Son of Man* in v.18 designates a significant way of looking at the life and work of Jesus. It pictures him as the victim of injustice and cruelty but also as the one to be raised *on the third day*. It presents his life and work as a contrast between humiliation and vindication, a contrast which is crucial to the final chapters of the Matthean narrative. Here the contrast is simply between humiliation and vindication; later it will be developed as a contrast between the one who is judged and the one who will be judge.

123

H. About Status
20.20–28

Like the first two predictions of the Passion and Resurrection, the
third is followed by a conversation between Jesus and his disciples.
The first concerned Peter's lack of understanding of the Son of Man's
mission (16.22–28), and the second concerned freedom from the
demands of earthly rulers (17.24–27). The third is about a place of
honour with the Son of Man as the end draws near; it is the narrative
of the request on behalf of the sons of Zebedee: *The mother of Zebedee's
sons then approached him with her sons* (v.20). In Mark the sons
approach Jesus alone; in Matthew it is the mother who speaks for
them. She requests *'that in your kingdom these two sons of mine may sit
next to you, one at your right hand and the others at your left'* (v.21). It is
not clear whether this is a direct request for status, or if it is a desire to
stand in the eternal courts as the Son of Man's attendants and
supporters. The second is attractive in view of what has been said
about heaven in Matthew 19.28 (see also 18.19: 'if two of you agree on
earth about any request you have to make, that request will be
granted'). In either case, the answer given to the brothers is that
what they ask is beyond their comprehension (an interesting side-
light on 18.20). To indicate how little they have understood of his
mission, Jesus asks if they can drink the cup which he is about to
drink (v.22). There are two interesting features of that saying: first,
the cup refers to Jesus' own future fate, and although that fate could
be seen in terms of either suffering or triumph, in this context vv. 18f.
have suggested that he will suffer unjust judgement and death (see
Isaiah 51.17 and Psalm 75.8); second, the Marcan reference to
baptism is absent from Matthew. In Mark Jesus uses baptism in a
figurative sense, asking the two sons of Zebedee if they can be
baptized with his baptism; Matthew does not use baptism in a
figurative sense, reserving the word for the declaration of Christ's
obedient sonship at his baptism by John with its promise of world-
wide salvation, and for the distinctively Christian sign of Christ's
lordship and sovereignty at baptism into the threefold name for all
who learn and practise Christ's way. The two disciples protest that
they are willing to share his fate, but Jesus even so can make no
promise. He detaches their willingness to suffer with him from any
sharing in his ultimate glory (v.23). *'That honour is for those to
whom it has already been assigned by my Father.'*

124

At this point the position of vv.20–28 within Matthew becomes significant. Not only does it follows the third prediction, it also follows the parable of the Workers in the Vineyard. It picks up several features of the preceding parable. Like the parable, the request to Jesus concerns positions of honour: who is first and who is lowest (19.30; 20.16,27). It also contains a vigorous argument between those aggrieved at the request. The ten disciples turn on the two brothers (v.24): *When the other ten heard this, they were indignant with the two brothers.* So Jesus has to remind them of the values in his kingdom. Earthly rulers control the lives of their subjects (the REB translation '*lord it over*' suggests a superior attitude rather than, as the original does, their absolute authority). That is the opposite of the Son of Man's pattern of life and work. The Son of Man does not bind people as slaves to masters; he suffers in order to deliver people from what enslaves them. So those who follow him (v.26) will understand greatness in terms of service not control. Delivering the people from what enslaves them involves him in giving his life *as a ransom for many* (v.28). Ransom in this context means a freely offered life given as a means of releasing other lives under forfeit (IV Maccabees 6.28). What enslaves and has enslaved the people over many generations is false leadership. This has distorted the people's life and brought it under the judgement of God. The Old Testament presents many pictures of a people's release from enslavement through the work of a group or individual. There are the pictures of a chosen few, of a righteous remnant, and of a Messiah. And, stressing the suffering involved, Matthew has already used Isaiah 42.1–4 (see Matthew 12.18–21) and Isaiah 53.4 (see Matthew 8.17) of an individual who has brought healing and hope by humiliating service and by suffering what others have brought on themselves. Now, in the picture of ransom, it becomes evident that only a life laid down will effect the release, and here is an individual able and ready to pay the price. That individual moreover brings hope to the Gentiles, for the latter too are under divine judgement because of their cruelty and idolatry. So when we read that the Son of Man gives his life *as a ransom for many*, several aspects of his self-offering are brought to mind; it is clear that 'the many' means a very large number – the people, the Gentiles; some would argue that it means 'all', since that is the meaning of the corresponding phrase in Isaiah 53.

I. The Son of David
20.29–34

These pictures of an individual who brings hope to the nation are gathered together again in the following story. In both Matthew and Mark the Son of Man is addressed in his Davidic or messianic status and he takes on the role of a merciful healer. It is the Solomonic tradition of messiahship which dominates here, not the conquering warlike picture, but there is a strong indication of the messianic passages which are to come. *Two blind men sit at the roadside* as the crowd leaves Jericho on the last lap of the journey to Jerusalem. Hearing that Jesus is passing by, they call on him for mercy (v.30). Just as the disciples had earlier tried to prevent the children from coming to Jesus, the crowd try to restrain the blind men (v.31). But they will not be silenced, and cry out again *'Have pity on us, Son of David.'* Nothing and no one can exclude the weak and vulnerable from his compassion. Several of the features of the Marcan story are absent from Matthew. What is preserved has a single point. The blind ask him for what they need and he answers their request (v.32); in compassion he heals their blindness. The story ends with the two men joining the huge crowd as followers of Jesus in their progress to Jerusalem.

§12 Jesus Enters Jerusalem
21.1–22.46

A. The Entry
21.1–11

21.1 *They were approaching Jerusalem.* Chapter 21 introduces rearrangements of order in Matthew over against the order of events in Mark. Matthew has the Entry into Jerusalem (with the messianic entry in lowly majesty, 21.1–9), The Cleansing of the Temple and the Messianic Healings in the Temple (21.10–16), and the Return to Bethany (21.17). Mark has the Entry, the Return to Bethany, the Cursing of the Fig Tree, the Cleansing of the Temple, and the Message of the Fig Tree, in that order. The change of order may not seem particularly significant. But the result of the reordering in Matthew is fundamental. In Mark the impression is given that a prophetic proclamation of punishment on Jerusalem has begun. The fig tree has been cursed and has already begun to wither. In Matthew the addition of the messianic healings after the cleansing of the temple introduces a new factor: it adds to the prophecy of destruction a prophecy of hope. So the change of order reminds us of the historical setting of Matthew's gospel. When Jesus had been teaching, Jerusalem was a great city of pilgrimage. Jews who had been scattered across the world (the Diaspora) returned, three times in the year, if they were able to do so, for the Festivals of Passover, Weeks and Tabernacles. Herod's temple was the place of sacrifice, the place of the Holy of Holies, and its high priests were honoured as mediating the divine presence. The reality of the aristocracy's work was however divisive because of its treatment of the poor; as far as Roman authority was concerned it was eventually ineffective; and as far as the fulfilment of the law was concerned it was too much involved with the fine detail to preserve its substance. Jesus' entry into Jerusalem and his prophecy of the cleansing of the temple would have been deeply threatening to Judaism.

By the time the gospel of Mark came to be written the temple was about to be or had already been destroyed. The horrific days of the Jewish War were crowding in or were a recent and painful memory, and Jesus' prophecy of cleansing was being witnessed as a total destruction. The power of Rome had exercised its authority and disaster had followed. By Matthew's time all that was past history; Jerusalem had fallen; the movement of refugees from Jerusalem into the Diaspora had caused the kind of disruption which we witness all too often today, and new Jewish communities had developed in and around major cities. The temple tax (see §9F) had been taken over by Rome. Yet Jerusalem itself remained a symbol of Jewish faith and hope. The study of the texts on sacrifice became for some Jews almost a form of divine worship in itself, and the work of scribes and those at the newly constituted centre at Javneh (Jamnia) continued the search for divine truth. Against that background we can see how the entry of Jesus into Jerusalem and his cleansing of the temple would have been seen in different ways. The order of the Matthean narrative is therefore significant. It points to a fresh perspective on the events of Jesus' lifetime. The Messiah enters to cleanse the temple and reaffirm the promises of God for the future, bringing hope to all. Jesus asks the disciples to go into a nearby village (Bethphage?) and find a *donkey tethered with her foal beside her* (v.2). The planning of the entry shows it to be a parallel to the dramatic actions of Old Testament prophets: *'The Master needs them'* (v.3). He is about to demonstrate in Jerusalem the nature of his mission. It is moreover a fulfilment of a prophecy. In contrast to the entry of great rulers of the past, like Alexander the Great, who rode on horseback into the cities they had taken, this 'king' would come *'in gentleness, riding on a donkey, on the foal of a beast of burden'* (v.5).

Here we come across another feature of Matthew which differs from Mark's account. In Mark the Old Testament background to the triumphal entry is implicit. In Matthew it is explicit; Matthew quotes directly from Zechariah 9.9 (in a form slightly different from our LXX version and linked with phrases from Isaiah 62.1). The quotation contains the key phrase *in gentleness* (so the REB; some translate the word 'lowly' or 'humble'). It is the lowly Messiah who enters the royal city. The text of Zechariah 9.9 might suggest that two animals, a donkey and its colt, were to be brought. Some scholars, fearing that such a suggestion must imply that Matthew did not know Hebrew, (he had not recognized that the Hebrew parallelism – on a donkey, on the foal – indicated a single animal), argue that Matthew must have made the inference from Mark's description of the donkey used by Jesus: no one had ever ridden on it. The argument illustrates how difficult it becomes when we try to explain every divergence of Matthew from Mark as the work of a single editor. It is much more likely that the shift to two animals took place in a context much earlier than Matthew's. The disciples do as they have been instructed (v.6). The crowds put their cloaks on the roadway (see II Kings 9.13), spreading branches cut from the trees (v.8), and the cry goes up *'Hosanna to the Son of David! Blessed is he who comes in the name of the Lord! Hosanna in the heavens!'* (v.9). The Messiah enters Jerusalem on a colt to the acclamations of the accompanying crowd (Hosanna is a festival acclamation, linking the prayer for salvation with praise for God's faithfulness; it is a welcome to the Son of David, and an act of praise to God); and he brings a new hope of healing for Judaism (see Psalm 118.19–29) and for all people. The act of cleansing which is to follow may already be heralded in the acclamation 'Blessed is he who comes in the name of the Lord.' Those words are retained by Matthew in 23.39 and can only there refer to judgement day. A sense of excitement in the city is vividly expressed by the REB (v.10) as those in the city ask who this is, and the accompanying crowd respond *'This is the prophet Jesus, from Nazareth in Galilee'* (v.11).

B. *The Temple Cleansed*
21.12–13

Lowly the Messiah may be, but the prophetic drama of his entry into Jerusalem culminates in another dramatic action, this time of violence. He cleanses the temple (v.12). Jesus *drove out all who were buying and selling in the temple precincts.* The reference is to the arrangements made in the Gentile court of the temple for normal currency to be turned into Tyrian currency for the payment of the temple tax, and for the sale of birds and animals required for sacrifice. The action is not intended to prevent the proper fulfilment of the law; it signals the cleansing of the temple from unjust controls and exchanges. There is again a significant difference between Mark's account and the account of Matthew and Luke. In all three gospels Jesus associates his action with a prophecy from Isaiah 56.7 and Jeremiah 7.11 (where those who cry 'The temple of the Lord', thinking themselves to be safe, are to be judged for turning the holy place into a robbers' cave). But in quoting from Isaiah 56.7, Jesus in Mark's gospel refers to the temple as a 'place of prayer for all nations'. In Matthew and Luke 'for all nations' is omitted. The temple, as a building, is for Judaism; and by the time of Matthew and Luke it has disappeared. The cleansing of the temple therefore becomes a prophecy of judgement, but also of hope; and in Matthew's time that symbol of hope is to be reaffirmed (see vv.14–17).

C. Healing in the Temple
21.14–17

21.14   *In the temple the blind and the crippled came to him and he healed them.* The healings in the temple are greeted by children's hosannas. For the children grasp the importance of what is happening there. The Messiah has come to offer cleansing and healing to the people, and 'the children in the temple' like the 'little ones' of chs. 18 and 19 are open to that divine truth (see §10A). By contrast the chief priests and scribes *were indignant* (v.15) and remonstrate with Jesus: *'Do you hear what they are saying?'* (v.16). The quotation which Jesus offers in reply is from the LXX of Psalm 8.3 (REB 8.2 is a translation of that verse from the Hebrew): *You have made children and babes at the breast sound your praise.'* Jesus leaves them and goes to Bethany.

D. The Fig Tree
21.18–22

21.18   *Next morning on his way* to Jerusalem Jesus sees a *fig tree* (v.19). He is hungry, but the tree carries only *leaves.* He curses it and it withers immediately. In Mark the story depicts Israel coming under judgement because it does not bear fruit appropriate to the time of the Messiah's arrival. It has been given the opportunity of repentance and has failed. The cursing of the fig tree in Matthew 21.18–22 lacks that focus; it becomes instead an illustration of the power of faith. The issue of faith, particularly the role of faith in miracles of

130

healing, has played a key role in earlier Matthean narratives. Even if faith is as small as a mustard seed, it can have extraordinary results (17.20). In 17.20 the fallibility of the disciples was fully recognized; it was the presence of the healer which was all important. The results promised in 21.21 are extraordinary indeed: mountains can be hurled into the sea. Jesus is as usual employing extreme pictures. It is important also that there is no mention here of 'little faith'? Faith in this case is partly defined by the phrase 'and have no doubts': *'if only you have faith and have no doubts, you will do what has been done to the fig tree'* (v.21). It is not only the extreme pictures which highlight Jesus' point about miracles – the mountains being thrown into the sea; it is the extreme language which he uses here about faith. He challenges the disciples to a faith well beyond what they possess. In v.22 the promise that prayers will be heard is made yet again (see 7.7; 18.19), this time associated specifically with faith: *'Whatever you pray for in faith you will receive.'* During the course of this commentary several comments have been made about the nature of faith and its relation to miracles. Perhaps the most important of these stresses the centrality of seeking the will of God (26.39. see 9.29 and § 4F). In 20.21 the request failed that test (§11H). There is a realism about Matthew's gospel; it accepts the narratives about faith and miracles but it places them in the context of the responsible doing of God's will (see 7.21).

E. By What Authority?
21.23–27

At this moment in the narrative Jesus begins teaching in the temple. Jesus had entered the city again (v.23) on the day after the cleansing of the temple. As he teaches the question is raised about the authority by which he acts (v.23): *'Who gave you this authority?'* At first sight it seems that Jesus evades the question (vv.24–27b). The reality is in fact somewhat different. Even the apparent evasion contains an implied answer; and the subsequent controversies all centre on that same subject: by what authority does Jesus teach and act? Earlier, Jesus had associated himself closely with John the Baptist. They shared the same message, the same senseless treatment from Jewish leaders, the same positive responses from sinners and the same vocation as representatives of the divine wisdom. Now Jesus makes use of that association to suggest how the question of authority can be understood: '*I also have a question for you . . .*' he says to the priests and elders: '*The baptism of John: was it from God, or from men?*' (v.25). The question raised by the priests and elders was born of an unwillingness to face reality. It was the original question which was an evasion, not Jesus' answer. The question revealed an unwillingness to face the truth about God's work in John the Baptist and Jesus. '*If we say "From God"*', argue the priests and elders, he will say, '*Then why did you not believe him?*' (v.25). So they answered: '*We do not know*' (v.26).

F. Sinners Come First (the Two Sons)
21.28–32

21.28 *There was a man who had two sons.* The parable of the Two Sons is a puzzle, perhaps intentionally so. One of its puzzles need not be attempted here, since the REB gives no hint of it; there is an amazing variety of textual variations involving the answers each son gave. We can therefore concentrate on the puzzle in the REB text. Having heard how each of the sons reacted to the father's request, we might well ask: '*Which of the two did what the father wanted?*' (v.31). The solution proposed in 21.31b–32 is unexpected: the one who can admit a mistake and correct it! That is something which the Jewish leaders (and by no means only the Jewish leaders) could not do. The parallel is drawn with the immoral arch-collaborators, the *tax-collectors and prostitutes*. John the Baptist came showing the way of righteousness (either, as in the Jerusalem Bible, 'himself a pattern of righteousness', or as the REB *to show you the right way to live*). They admitted their mistakes and corrected them (v.32); *they enter* the kingdom ahead of you (the chief priests and elders) (v.31). The theme of rejection and replacement now becomes of central importance. Those who expected to enter the kingdom remain outside; those who had no such hope find that the door is opened. There is no security of entrance; and those who believe they have that security may be heading for disaster. It would be misleading to regard this as an attack on Israel only, or even on the Jewish leaders only. Those who have been invited, whether Jew or Gentile, have to take note of the warning: beware of barren branches!

G. Rejects and Replacements (the Vineyard)
21.33–46

As we have seen, the question concerning the authority of Jesus (v.23) governs the material up to 22.46. It is answered in surprising ways. The first apparent evasion of the question turns out to be a powerful reply. Then three following parables and four conflict-stories reveal further answers, each of great depth and intensity. The three parables (21.28–22.14) contribute a common theme to that answer: there will be unexpected entrants into the kingdom who will replace those who expect a place. The parable of the Wicked Tenants (21.33–43) is the second of the three parables. Its conclusion warns that a new obedient people will take the place of those who revolt against God and his Son. The parable itself is about a vineyard on which an owner has lavished great care (v.33), and about tenants who go to extreme lengths in denying the owner his lawful rights (vv.34–39); as a result they are themselves displaced. Those three features of the parable all correspond to elements in the story of Jesus. God has lavished great care on Israel; the Jewish leaders have rejected all God's representatives, including finally Jesus himself ('. . . *when they saw the son the tenants said to one another, "This is the heir; come on, let us kill him, and get his inheritance"* ', v.38); they will therefore be displaced in favour of those *who will give him his share of the crop when the season comes* (v.41). The quotation from Psalm 118.22–23 in 21.42 was used by the early church to underline the seriousness of rejecting Christ (I Peter 2.7). Both Matthew and Luke highlight this in various ways. That is true of Matthew 21.44: '*Any man who falls on this stone will be dashed to pieces; and if it falls on a man he will be crushed by it.*' But translations often place this verse in the margin (see the REB) because some editors are uncertain whether or not it belongs to the original text of Matthew. Whatever may be the judgement of the editors, v.44 agrees with the tenor of the whole passage. The conclusion therefore runs: '. . . *I tell you, the kingdom of God will be taken away from you, and given to a nation that yields the proper fruit*' (v.43). Once again the saying gives the appearance of being directed wholly against the Jewish leadership (vv.45f.). But the qualification in v.43, *that yields the proper fruit* means that everyone must take care. The exact meaning of 'yielding fruit' will not be wholly apparent until the end of the final discourse, although much has already been said about it (see §3L). But whatever it means, it sets up a requirement for entry into the kingdom which all who wish to enter that kingdom must note.

H. Guests at the Feast
22.1–14

Jesus again uses parables (v.1): *The kingdom of Heaven is like this. There was a king who arranged a banquet for his son's wedding* (v.2). The parable of the Feast continues the theme of 'replacement'. The royal wedding feast is ready, but not one of the invited guests is willing to attend (v.3). A second reminder to the guests produces an even stronger reaction (v.6; the parallels with the Wicked Tenants are interesting here); they react violently and their violence brings down the wrath of the king (v.7). So finally servants are sent out to invite in anyone who will come, good and bad alike, and these fill the banquet hall (v.10). The significance of the parable is clarified by the meals which Jesus shared with his friends, in two ways. It is characteristic of the meals of Jesus that he ate with publicans and sinners. It was his way of demonstrating acceptance of them. The meal made them welcome, whoever they were. So it is entirely appropriate that in the parable of the Feast the newly invited guests should include the bad as well as the good. All were welcome at the feast. There is another feature of the parable which is clarified by comparison with the final meal which Jesus ate with his disciples. The final meal pointed forward to the messianic banquet. It was an anticipation of the future celebration of God's final victory. The parable of the Feast shared the same kind of expectation. The wedding of the king's son was a parable of the last days, of the gathering together of God's people to share in his joy. The final section of the parable comes therefore as something of a surprise. All have been made welcome; the feast is ready; the hall is full; the celebration begins. Then the host discovers someone without a wedding garment (v.11); and when the offender is discovered he is speechless (v.12) and is punished not just by expulsion from the feast but by being thrown out into the dark, *the place of wailing and grinding of teeth* (v.13). The traditional explanation is that the wedding garment stands for 'good works'; the clue to the parable is then that the king's welcome carries with it responsibilities, which if they are not fulfilled can result in disaster. On those grounds to be invited to the feast is not enough: *For many are invited, but few are chosen* (v.14). The ferocity of the punishment belongs to a significant Old Testament tradition. The Deuteronomic tradition uses the language of destruction and darkness, and in Matthew's gospel that language is given a new context. The city which is destroyed is Jerusalem; those who are thrown into darkness

I. Four Conflicts: 1 Taxes
22.15–22

Pharisees and Herodians now set a *trap* (v.15). It is one of four typical problems set for Jesus. The four Matthean conflict stories are similar to those in Mark; but they differ from Mark in their emphases. In the first the question is about taxes: '. . . *are we or are we not permitted to pay taxes to the Roman emperor?*' (v.17). In the Matthean narrative the coin is presented to Jesus (v.19) and its significance is discussed (vv.20f.), with two main emphases: on the wickedness of the questioners (v.18: *their malicious intention*) and on the compatibility between what Jesus says here and the previous discussion of taxation in 17.24–27. The response of Jesus is strikingly ambiguous: '*Then pay to Caesar what belongs Caesar, and to God what belongs to God.*' That can mean either that payment to Caesar includes a proper recognition of God or that Caesar and God control separate unrelated realms. In Matthew's gospel there is no incitement to revolt. That is clear from the reaction of his questioners; the result of the discussion in vv.15–22 is that his questioners back off (v.22). They have no immediate cause for complaint. On the other hand Matthew's material has a cutting edge. It consistently paints the great rulers of the world as tyrannical and oppressive. The emperor is no exception, and God sets a clear limit to such exercise of power. One such limit is the freedom enjoyed by those who are 'children of the kingdom'. There is a close correspondence with 17.24–27, where Jesus agrees pays the tax to avoid offence but in principle claims exemption for all God's people. The narrative has often been quoted in relation to contemporary discussions of civil liberty: in the matter of a poll-tax should government decisions be obeyed? The contemporary situation is different in so far as the political system is relatively democratic, and the responsibilities which are enjoyed and shared link members of society together today in ways which Matthew and his communities would never have known. The right of conscience remains, but needs to be tested in public debate and in the courts of law.

J. Four Conflicts: 2 The Resurrection
22.23–33

The second conflict is with the Sadducees (v.23). The position of the
Sadducees at the time of Jesus and at the time of Matthew is briefly
discussed in §2B. What is important here is that the Sadducees deny
that there is an after-life and make their case by means of contemporary marriage law (v.24). Jesus answers them with a quotation
from Exodus 3.6: *'I am the God of Abraham, the God of Isaac, the God of
Jacob'* (v.32). At first sight the answer of Jesus appears to be in-
nocuous. It seems to rest solely on an association of Abraham, Isaac
and Jacob with the verb 'I am': 'I am (now as well as I was long ago)
the God of Abraham, Isaac and Jacob.' But the quotation does not
stand alone. It is accompanied by the basic principle stated in v.32b:
'God is not God of the dead but of the living.' That is where the argument
rests; God is a God of power (v.29) and that power is able to make
alive and sustain life. It is on account of this power that God is and
remains the God of Abraham, Isaac and Jacob. He is the one who
ensures their continued existence. The precise meaning of this
declaration for Matthew is not certain. But there is sufficient
evidence from the time of Matthew to warrant the view that
Abraham, Isaac and Jacob could have been understood to be in the
presence of God, sharing the heavenly existence of angels and
martyrs of the past. The argument of Jesus, when transposed into
that context, has an additional force: God is the God of the living.
Matthew, like Luke, notes the effectiveness of Jesus' reply (v.33).

K. Four Conflicts: 3 The Commandments
22.34–40

Third, again as part of the Pharisees' plot, Jesus is drawn into a
discussion with a scribe concerning *the greatest commandment of the law*
(v.36). According to the scribe it is Deuteronomy 6.5, accompanied
by Leviticus 19.18: the injunction to love God and the injunction to
love one's neighbour. In Matthew these two passages are given a
central place in the understanding of all the law and the prophets.
What that central place is we find in v.40: *Everything in the law and
the prophets hangs on these two commandments.* But v.40 may mean
that these two commands provide firm pegs on which the law and

prophets can hang; they provide the law and the prophets with a
secure position. Or alternatively v.40 could mean that they provide
the fixed point from which all the law and prophets can be drawn
out; all the law and prophets can be deduced from them or traced to
them. Probably both interpretations are helpful. The law and the
prophets indicate all that God requires and the means for interpreting God's commandments. The two injunctions are statements of a
basic morality, fundamental in every respect to God's requirements.
They are foundational, a focus, a summary; they are maxims of a
deeper significance than all others, going to the heart of what God
requires (see 7.12; §3K). The combination of Deuteronomy 6.5 and
Leviticus 19.18 is important in another way: that particular combination is found in Jewish-Hellenistic texts, and whatever its origin
might be, forms part of an attempt to give the law as a whole a
universal authority. It is true that attempts were made to identify
parts of the law which were of universal validity by virtue of the
Covenant with Noah. But this combination here, presented in relation to the whole of the law and the prophets, presents the universal
validity not only of a part of the law but goes to the heart of all that
God requires. The significance of all the verse continues long after
Matthew's time. In dealing with so many contemporary issues
today, especially those which affect decisions on health and medical
technology, the vital issue is to find standpoints which are widely
accepted across races and cultures.

L. *Four Conflicts: 4 The Messiah*
22.41–46

In the last of the confrontations Jesus takes the initiative (v.41). In
Matthew's version the confrontation is with the Pharisees. Jesus asks
them about the Messiah: *'Whose son is he?'*; and they provide a clear
statement of the Davidic origin for the Messiah: *'The son of David'*. It is
as if the writer wishes that statement to be made as clearly as
possible. In Mark the issue is left to inference. Not so in Matthew. In
Matthew the Pharisees themselves affirm it. But side by side with
that affirmation Jesus places a quotation from Psalm 110.1: 'This is
the Lord's oracle to my Lord, "Sit at my right hand, and I shall make
your enemies your footstool" ' (v.44). The quotation is understood as
from the mouth of David, who records a promise given by the Lord
(i.e. God) to David's Lord (i.e. the Messiah). The Messiah is to be

made Lord over all. From the quotation Jesus draws the inference that the Messiah must be superior to David. Jesus then asks the question how in that case the Messiah could be David's son (v.45). This conclusion to the discussion between Jesus and the Pharisees is not explained. There is no need, since it silences his hearers. Perhaps Matthew implies that there is a richness to the messianic hope which defies political and nationalistic categories. Jesus is not to be restricted to those limits. He may be messiah in the line of David, but there is much more that needs to be said than that, and the narratives which have been assembled provide the evidence.

§13 The Final Address (Discourse 5)
23.1–25.46

A. On Scribes and Pharisees
23.1–12

23.1 *Jesus then addressed the crowds and his disciples in these words.*
Where does the fifth and final discourse begin? Perhaps ch. 23 is
already a part of it, making a long section, chs. 23–25. Certainly if
Matthew is based upon Mark, Mark provides the key structural
elements for all three chapters. But then again perhaps the final
discourse only begins at 24.1, and ch. 23 is a separate unit. Whatever
the answer to that particular structural problem, ch. 23 begins with
an unexpected comment. Jesus compliments the scribes: *The scribes
and the Pharisees occupy Moses' seat; so be careful to do whatever they tell
you* (vv.2–3a). They carry the authority of Moses as instructor and
guide, and they are reliable interpreters of the law. This is the basis of
13.52 (see §7C). The scribal tradition was an ancient one in Israel and
the ancient Near East. Ecclesiasticus 38.24–39.11 tells of such a
scribe. It describes the wisdom of the scribe, which fits him for
responsibility in the courts and in the local assemblies, and comes
from his study of the law and of all other kinds of knowledge. It
describes also his spirituality, his dependence on the Lord's wisdom
for inspiration, so that he can give thanks to the Lord in prayer and
understand parables, prophetic utterances and divine mysteries.
Matthew's gospel shows evidence of the work of such scribes and
shows approval of them. In addition to 13.52 and 23.3 there is an
important commendation in 23.34 which the REB translation has
hidden: 23.34 should be translated 'I (Wisdom) am sending you
therefore prophets, and wise men and scribes.' The trouble is that, as
Matthew's gospel sees it, some of the Pharisaic scribes (as distinct
from scribes associated with other groups in Judaism) do not illustrate in the way they live the quality of their profession: *but do not
follow their practice* (v.36). So on the one hand the scribes are

commended warmly and positively; on the other the chapter mounts an attack on the Pharisaic scribes of great ferocity because they fail to live out the truth. Examples of their unacceptable behaviour follow (vv. 4–7): they lay *heavy burdens* on people. Is this a result of failing to show the humility which Jesus shows (see 11.28–30), or of not making justice and mercy priorities (see §6D)? They wear *broad phylacteries* (the small boxes containing four texts from the law) and *large tassels* on the corner of their garments (see Deuteronomy 22.12). They anticipate preferential treatment at dinners, in synagogues, and in the street (see 6.2), and they enjoy the title '*rabbi*'. The significance of this last criticism rests on the growing importance in Matthew's time of the rabbinic teacher, and also in the contrast between those who love and those who reject honorific titles: '*But you must not be called "rabbi", for you have one Rabbi, and you are all brothers*' (v.8). There are Christian denominations whose constitutions are determined by this verse. They understand it literally and shape their life by it. It is never easy to hold a group of people together without a structure in which individuals are designated by titles, and the picture which is presented here is remarkably different from 16.18f. and 18.18. (Was not Peter required to be Teacher and Leader? See v.10.) Perhaps Matthew recognized that the material in 23.8–12 would be relevant whatever constitution a Christian community operated. Matthean communities had leaders, interpreters, scribes, instructors, perhaps some even had a bishop. Undoubtedly they valued those who fulfilled such functions. The development of the community depended on them. But to fulfil the function was one thing; to allow the function to become a means to personal prestige was quite another. The function needed to be fulfilled in humility and in dependence on God and his Messiah. Certainly Jesus would not have expected literal obedience to the direction in v.9: '*Do not call any man on earth "father", for you have one Father, and he is in heaven.*' But he would expect his warning to be taken seriously ('*The greatest among you must be your servant*', *v.11*) and applied to practical relationships. So Matthew is aware that humility can be exercised in any role (see v.12), and the apparently unimportant roles may well prove in the end to be the most essential.

B. The Woes
23.13–33

The ferocity of the attack which follows is almost without parallel in the gospels. Seven sections open with the word 'Woe!' or 'Alas!', i.e. 'How tragic it would be if . . .' and in some of them the language is abusive. The term *hypocrite* itself carries a severe judgement (see 6.1 and §3H). The First Woe is an attack on leaders who use the keys intended for aiding entry into the kingdom to lock people out: '*You shut the door of the kingdom of Heaven in people's faces; you do not enter yourselves, and when others try to enter, you stop them*' (v.13). At the literal level it is not clear how this can be reconciled with approval of Peter's powers in 16.19. He can exclude some by the power of the keys. It can be argued that Peter is authorized to exclude some and would of course be entering the kingdom himself. But the problem still remains of using the power of the keys to lock the gates instead of unlocking them. Peter can do that for which the Jewish leaders are criticized. Perhaps the Woe is not intended to be heard at a literal level; it is another example of picturesque, exaggerated speech. But what then is its force? As Jesus intended it the saying would have recognized the contribution which scribes made to the understanding of the divine will, yet their practice had obscured it for many, caused many to be estranged from the truth, and put themselves at risk.

23.15   The Second Woe, takes that line of argument further: '*You travel over sea and land to win one convert* (literally 'proselyte'); *and when you have succeeded you make him twice as fit for hell as you are yourselves.*' By contrast Matthew would have seen this as warning his contemporary Jewish leaders against seeking back proselytes who had linked up with Christian communities. 'Over sea and land' illustrates the gaps in our knowledge of first-century Judaism. We have no secure information, although some imaginative constructions have been made, about international mission work by Pharisees. In any case it is an example of exaggerated speech: 'You expend endless effort, and what is the end result!' Several of the 'Woes' warn against false perspectives.

23.16   The Third Woe takes up the subject of oaths (see §3E), but whereas 5.33–37 was concerned about the devaluing of holiness through evasion and lying, 23.16–22 attacks the minute distinctions in which the centrality of God is forgotten. Oaths are binding ultimately because of God. It is he who provides the criteria for judging what is true and what is false. So when oaths are used to evade the truth, the answer is not to define what is the more binding, *gold* or *sanctuary* (v.16), *altar* or sacrifice (v.17). They are too intimately linked; above all they are linked in a sequence in which what is holy can be traced back to the holiness of God. (vv.21f.).

23.23   In the Fourth Woe false perspectives are attacked. Small details of practice, the tithing of *mint*, *dill* and *cummin*, as an extension of Deuteronomy 14.22–29, are given a high profile, while major concerns such as *justice, mercy and good faith* are overlooked. That is not say that tithing is unimportant. But it is to say that tithing is peripheral whereas *justice, mercy, and good faith* (v.23) are central. The picture which drives this particular shaft home is unforgettable: these are blind guides who would *strain off a midge and gulp down a camel!* (v.24).

23.25   The Fifth Woe is variously translated: REB gives a translation which criticizes the scribes and Pharisees for debating about what makes a cup ceremonially clean: whether the inside and outside of a cup should be cleaned or only the inside; the central debate should not be about cups but be about whether a person is inwardly clean. TEV translates it: full of what you have gotten by violence and selfishness. The TEV translation is the more accurate and the harsher of the two. Its harshness can only be justified if there is some truth in the other Woe which is often omitted from the text of Matthew and which appears in the REB margin as v.14: *Alas for you, scribes and Pharisees, hypocrites! You eat up the property of widows, while for appearance' sake you say long prayers.*

23.27   The Sixth Woe goes further still. It accuses the scribes and Pharisees of a contaminating lawlessness. They are *tombs covered with whitewash*, that is, they are marked every year at festival time so that the unwary passer-by might not be defiled by them. Externally they look good; inside they are full of corruption (v.27). Externally they have the appearance of being righteous people; internally they have no respect for the law they claim to uphold (v.28).

23.29   The biting sarcasm of the final and Seventh Woe brings the sequence to a close. It resembles the language and style of John the

Baptist. Like the Baptist Jesus mocks his opponents and calls them a *'vipers' brood'* (v.33). The seventh 'Woe' is about prophets, wise men and scribes. The current generation might as well get on with the task left unfinished by their predecessors and kill off all the prophets (v.32). Outwardly they make a show of honouring the prophets (vv.29f.); in fact they are killing them off. The sarcasm of this passage might seem out of character with the Jesus of our traditional reconstructions. But before we ascribe the material to Matthean attitudes to Jewish leaders we should note the equally sharp irony of the parallel passage in Luke (Luke 11.47f.). That does not of course mean that the ferocity of language must go back to Jesus. It could belong to a tradition shared by Matthew and Luke. But it could also be that Jesus and John the Baptist, in speaking of the inevitability of judgement, used the same violent terms.

C. *The New Mission*
23.34–39

The opening words of this section *'I am sending you . . .'* (v.34) could be taken in a weak or a strong sense. If their meaning is 'And so . . .' then the promise of prophets, wise men and scribes signals the beginning of a fresh wave of violence. If the opening words are intended to be strong, and they have the sense of *therefore*, as in the REB, then the sentence has a more sinister ring. Not only does the sending of God's messengers signal an outbreak of violence, it is intended to provoke that outbreak. *Therefore* indicates that the decision to send the fresh wave of messengers is consequent on the earlier murders and is intended to implicate the current generation. This is hostile language, of a piece with the earlier 'Woes'. Even more striking is the use of 'I' in the opening verse: 'Therefore I send to you'. In Luke the parallel names Wisdom as the one who sends: 'This is why the Wisdom of God said, "I will send them prophets and messengers" ' (Luke 11.49). In Matthew the one who takes on Wisdom's role in the sad history of successive persecutions is none other than Jesus. It is Jesus who provokes the outbreak of violence, so that (v.35; some translators such as the TEV again choose the weaker phrase 'with the result that'; REB has the ambiguous 'So') the current generation may reap its due reward. Its atrocities match the appalling persecutions in the course of Jewish history (Abel was the first in the Bible, Zechariah is the last – the Zechariah of the last book of the Hebrew Bible, II Chronicles 24.20–22, although he could be the prophet of Zechariah 1.1, or a son of Baruch whose murder is mentioned by the Jewish historian Josephus). Such atrocities cannot escape retribution. By persecuting God's messengers this generation admits its share in the inheritance of all the violence and murder of Israel's history. The ferocity of the language in this earlier part of the chapter is in marked contrast with the poignancy of what follows. Israel would not respond; yet Jesus was longing to shelter Jerusalem *as a hen gathers her brood under her wings*. All to no avail, it seems: *There is your temple, forsaken by God and laid waste* (v.38). And yet the chapter ends not with a threat but with a promise. It is a promise associated with another triumphant entry of Jesus: you will see me next only at *the time when you say, 'Blessed is he who comes in the name of the Lord'* (v.39).

D. Stages in the Future
24.1–36

Like its parallels in Mark and Luke this is a long discourse on the future. But to a greater extent than in those parallels the Matthean discourse concentrates on how much must happen before the end. Whatever else is said, the end cannot be soon:

(i)	Jerusalem will be destroyed	(v.2)
(ii)	False prophets	(v.4,11)
(iii)	All nations will go to war, will hate you	(vv.9–11)
	The gospel will be proclaimed through the earth	
(iv)	The abomination of desolation	(v.15)
(v)	Like lightning	(v.27)
(vi)	Cosmic disasters	(v.29)
(vii)	The Son of Man gathers the chosen	(v.31)
(viii)	Signs of the end	(v.33)
(ix)	Only the Father knows the time	(v.36)

Particularly important is (iii): The gospel must be proclaimed throughout the earth as a testimony to all nations. This anticipates the Great Commission at the end of this gospel where the disciples are sent out to make disciples of all nations, baptizing them in the name of Father, Son and Holy Spirit and teaching them all that Christ commanded. Mark has a similar interest (Mark 13.10), but in

144

Matthew the emphasis is very much greater. In the Matthean context v.14 seems to be saying: only then will the end come; in between are all the challenges to be met and the responsibilities to be fulfilled; and that should be the focus of your interests for the time being. Ch. 25 has three parables all of which sustain that focus, and warn that we have time, and the time we have should be used well. There will be plenty of opportunities to use and there are many mistakes which can be made.

(i) Jerusalem will be destroyed.

24.1–3   As Jesus walks away from the temple, the disciples point back to it, and Jesus prophesies that *not one stone will be left upon another*. So the disciples ask him in private about his *coming* and the *end of the age*.

(ii) False prophets.

24.4   One of the mistakes which might be made is listening to false prophets. That was made clear at the end of the Sermon on the Mount (7.15; see §3L), and this fifth and final discourse picks up the conclusion of the first discourse and draws out its importance. The warning about false messages is given twice in this passage. First there is the warning about those who will try to mislead the disciples (v.5: *For many will come claiming my name . . .*). It is closely parallel to both Mark and Luke. The false teaching is concerned with the coming of the Messiah and the rumours about various kinds of conflicts (v.6a). It is inevitable that wars will happen (v.6b). But not in the timescale suggested by the false teachers: *The end is still to come* (v.6c). These represent only a beginning, *birthpangs of the new age* (v.8). Second there is the warning of treachery. Accompanying and in part caused by the false teaching there will be a loss of mutual trust and care among the faithful (v.10). *Lawlessness* spreads (v.12): Again Matthew uses the word 'lawlessness'. It indicates the seriousness of this stage in the pattern of future events.

(iii) All nations.

24.14   *And this gospel of the kingdom will be proclaimed throughout the earth as a testimony to all nations . . .* It is very unlikely that the phrase 'throughout the earth' could exclude Palestine and the Jewish Diaspora (see 10.18; 24.9,16). The gospel is for all nations without

145

exception, both Jew and Gentile. All are to hear the good news. The extent of this commission should not be underestimated, nor would it have been underestimated by the hearers of Matthews' gospel. A long process is envisaged – 'to the end of the ages'.

(iv) The Abomination of Desolation.

24.15   There will be a need to escape from Judaea when '*the abomination of desolation' of which the prophet Daniel spoke* appears in the holy place. The reference is to Daniel 12.11 (LXX) and to the desecration of the altar of burnt offering in 168 BCE. However the phrase would also have been appropriate to Caligula's threat to place his image in the temple in 40CE, or to the setting up of military standards in the temple by Titus in 70CE. There is to be a sign bringing desolation in its wake because 'it' (in Matthew the abomination is not personalized, as it is in Mark) is a profound challenge to the holy place. Escape is necessary, as the disaster sweeps in. But escape from where? Vv.17f. suggest that the answer is: from Jerusalem and its environs, and it will require strength and speed. V.20 moves from general prophecy to direct address: '*Pray that it may not be winter or a sabbath when you have to make your escape.*' There have been adjustments to the tradition; these meet the circumstances of persecution which some Christians have endured. Jewish Christians would hesitate to travel on the sabbath or would fear intensified persecution from conservative Jews if they did. Two further passages from Daniel complete the section: the *great distress* will deepen (Daniel 12.1), a distress which thankfully will not be unending (v.22).

(v) Like Lightning

24.23–27   There is plenty of time for all this to happen; the end is not yet. That should not however lull the faithful into a false sense of security: *Impostors will come . . . producing great signs and wonders . . . to mislead, if possible, the chosen . . .* (v.24). The REB translation hides something of the turmoil behind this text. The original text speaks of 'false Christs' and 'false prophets'. These 'false prophets', taken along with the charges and countercharges about false prophecy to be found in Matthew's gospel – against Jesus (see Matthew 27.40), the disciples and adherents – suggest that there were in the time of Matthew serious problems about distinguishing true prophecy from

146

false (see Deuteronomy 13.1–3 regarding false prophets and signs). Matthew's criterion of 'doing the will of the heavenly Father' (7.21) is one of his contributions to the debate, together with his transformation of this massive end-of-time sequence in ch. 24 into an ultimate vision of vindication for those who do God's will. The sequence continues, and the end (vv.29–31), when it finally comes, will be self-evident, like lightning or circling eagles announcing a death (v.28).

(vi) Cosmic disaster.

24.29   Celestial disasters are pictured in language borrowed from Isaiah 13 and 34 where they signify the coming of God's judgement on the nations: *the sun will be darkened, the moon will not give her light; the stars will fall from the sky, the celestial powers will be shaken.* The role of such language is to heighten the moment of crisis; God is about to bring retribution on the earth, and the heavens signal the disaster.

(vii) The Son of Man gathers the chosen.

24.31   The trumpet-blast rings out between heaven and earth setting the last events in motion, and the angels draw together the chosen together. The phrase *from the four winds, from the farthest bounds of heaven on every side* differs from Mark's parallel in 13.27. TEV understands it to mean 'from one end of the world to the other'; *the farthest bounds of heaven* is a more literal translation and might imply the 'dead' as well as the 'living'.

(viii) Signs of the end.

24.34   Mark's parable of the Fig Tree is repeated by Matthew, along with the promise that *the present generation will live to see it all* (v.34). The parable could simply draw on the traditional imagery of new growth pointing to the summer season. But why is the summer season chosen and why the choice of the fig tree? The closest association with the subject matter of the end of time would be summer growth pointing toward harvest, rather than early growth pointing toward the summer. However the word used for 'summer' at this point in each of the gospels is used metaphorically of the heavenly paradise; and the choice of 'fig tree' might symbolize blessings in the end-time for the obedient. This would give the passage a meaning which throws a different light on the subject of end-time. Long-term responsibilities are important; but they are important not only for fear of a judgement but in expectation of great promise. The parable points to hope as well as judgement: *the end is near; at the very door.* The end-time holds out the possibilities of reward and bliss, as well as of judgement and punishment. The Fig Tree blessings and the vindication of courageous living are a new dawn and a new world.

APOCALYPTIC IN MATTHEW'S GOSPEL

Apocalyptic language is used in Matthew in several different ways. First, there is the language of judgement. This is used in four ways: of the past (24.39; see also 22.7), of the imminent future, of the inauguration of judgement (see §2B), and of the final judgement. In some cases the same vocabulary is used, although the context of judgement has changed. Particularly important is the overlap between the teaching of John the Baptist and the teaching of Jesus (3.12; 13.41). These emphasize God's judgement at work in history and across the world. In some examples, the language is ambiguous; it is not clear when or how judgement takes place; these include the highly specific Woes on the villages, almost certainly an original feature of Jesus' teaching (10.15; 11.22; see 12.36) . In others the focus is on particularly significant moments, the flood, the coming of Jesus, and the end-time. Second, there is the language of recompense: the quotation 'I set before you a blessing and a curse' summarizes the opportunities and dangers of the task committed to Israel. On the one hand there is the promise of the land, the inheritance, life, rest and a great nation; on the other there is the fierceness of the threats, so often found in Matthean material: e.g. 'outer darkness' (8.12; 22.13; 25.30), 'weeping and gnashing of teeth'. Third, there is the language of revelation (10.26; 13.16; 13.35; see §§7B and 9A). The opening of heaven enables the mysteries of heaven to be known by those to whom they are revealed (Apocalypse comes from the Greek word for 'reveal'). Fourth, there is the language of contrast, either of groups (19.28), or of origins (13.26), often associated with what has often been described as a dualistic approach to the world (see §§6E and 7B). This includes in Matthew the contrast between Holy Spirit and evil spirits, between God / the Son of Man (with his angels) and the devil (with his: 25.41). Finally there is the language of cataclysmic events (see §§13D (vi), 14J, 15A).

It is important to ask of each of these kinds of apocalyptic language what their reference point may be. In particular we need to ask what their reference point was for the writer of the gospel. First, the language of judgement derives in part from the Q tradition (see 5.20,22,29; 6.15; 7.14,23). Some of these, as far as Matthew is concerned, may be hyperbolic, i.e. a form of exaggerated speech used to arouse the listeners' attention and attract a response. They mark the extreme seriousness of ethical decisions and actions. Some (e.g. 10.15; 11.22) belong, again as far as Matthew is concerned, within the tradition of prophetic warnings: specific failure to repent carries with it disaster, initially an imminent historical disaster such as that suffered by Sodom (which is no longer 'standing', 11.23), but also, above and beyond such historical disaster, there is the perspective of God's sovereignty over all time, history and creation ('the day of judgement'), which means that sooner or later all injustice will be seen for what it is and put right, with regard to both victims and their persecutors. Such apocalyptic language refers to history and to the world, except that it refers by inference to the everlasting values enshrined in the sovereignty of God. The longer the historical vindication of those values is delayed, as is the case in Matthew's gospel, the greater the importance attached to their unchanging validity. Second, the language of recompense belongs to the patterns of Old Testament Deuteronomic thought. When those patterns are placed in Matthew alongside mercy, meekness, tolerance and love for one's enemies, and when the reference point changes from Israel to the universal vista of Gentile hopes, the function of the language of recompense changes. The issues of land, possession, inheritance and people are transformed; fear gives way before the ultimacy of love, and the pictures of punishment give metaphorical intensity to ethical standards. Third, the language of revelation has practical as well as theological relevance. Its reference points are forms of leadership and human need, as well as the enlightenment of heart and mind as the individual and community search for the divine will. Fourth, the language of contrast receives in Matthew a powerful qualification. It is no longer a matter of those who are called as against those who are rejected, but rather of those who are chosen because of the justice, humility and integrity of their lives. Fifth, the language of vision is hardest to evaluate. It could be, as in the case of judgement language, the unmasking of principalities and powers; or it could be the reception of heaven's everlasting values; or it could have its focus in the person who spans heaven and earth. Sixth, the language of cataclysmic events belongs with the increasing vitality of description and narrative used to expound the sense of awe and majesty surrounding the beginnings of Christianity.

(ix) Only the Father knows the time.

24.36   There will be those who continue to look for that day as a future experience and as an earthly coming. There were many such among the groups from whom Matthew drew these apocalyptic traditions. For them and for those who might be tempted to slack there is the Marcan reminder: . . . *about that day and hour no one knows . . . not even the Son; no one but the Father alone* (v.36). It is maintained several times in Matthew that the disciples do not know the timing of the final hour. Here in a saying shared with Luke it is maintained that the Son himself does not know it. It is difficult to know how to take such a saying. Certainly there could be no stronger way of stating that the issue is in God's hands.

E. *The Days of Noah*
24.37–41

The end will be a long time coming. But the disciples should not be lulled into a sense that decisions and responsibilities are unimportant. That concern is reiterated by Matthew in various ways. The next three parables are a trilogy on the sustaining of concentration and attention, or as Jesus calls it 'watching'. 'Watching' means obedient readiness for the end, sustained as if through a night watch. There is an illustration from the time of Noah. Illustrated here is the all too ordinary carelessness and unthinking security evidenced by the contemporaries of Noah: *In the days before the flood they ate and drank and married, until the day that Noah went into the ark* (v.38). The metaphor of the flood awakens memories of 7.27: *they knew nothing until the flood came and swept them all away.* The pictures of the two men in the field and the two women grinding underlines the uncertainty of the time and the danger of being caught unready (vv.40f.)

F. *A Thief in the Night*
24.42–44

Two further parables continue the theme of 'watching'. There is the parable of the Thief (24.42–44) and the parable of the Two Servants (24.45–51). The first uses the picture of the burglar. When the burglar might come is an unknown factor. It could be at any time: . . . *if the householder had known at what time of night the burglar was coming, he would have stayed awake* (v.43). When the Son of Man will come is similarly unknown. No one can predict it. It is not revealed to anyone in advance. No one can know the time. A consequence is drawn from this. Since no one can know when the burglar or when the Son of Man will come, there is only one way to behave: to keep awake and 'watch'! Only so can disaster be averted, either the damage to house and property, or the disaster of being caught unprepared by the Son of Man. But what exactly is meant by 'watching'?

G. *The Two Servants*
24.45–51

The next parable offers one answer. The contrast in the parable of the Two Servants between the faithful and wise on the one hand and the wicked on the other will occur in similar terms in the next chapter. Using parallel language, Matthew and Luke depict two different states: promotion to full control of a household for a servant who is wise enough to be found trustworthy, contrasted with demotion and worse (see v.51!) for a bully and a glutton (v.49). 'Watching' implies a quality of obedience. It means caring for the members of the household, supplying them with food at the proper time (v.45), as distinct from using responsibility for one's own advantage and guided by whim and fancy. The pictures of the parable and the life of the faithful can be described in corresponding terms. 'Watching' has those practical implications.

151

H. The Ten Virgins
25.1–13

The parable of the Ten Virgins continues the theme of 'watching' and the warning that no one knows the day or hour (see v.13): *When the day comes, the kingdom of Heaven will be like this. There were ten girls, who took their lamps and went out to meet the bridegroom . . . At midnight there came a shout: 'Here is the bridegroom!'* (vv.1,6) But the main point of the parable introduces a new factor. That new factor is death. If as seems likely the 'dozing off to sleep' of the virgins hints at the intervention of death, limiting our time for obedience, then the issue of 'watching' becomes even more important: *As the bridegroom was a long time in coming, they all dozed off to sleep* (v.5). We must watch while we can. Death may intervene and death ends our efforts to fulfil the divine will. Paul confronted a related problem in I Thessalonians 4.15–17: some Christians will be alive at the Second Coming; some will be dead. Death, presented as sleep, may intervene between now and the Bridegroom's call. If this is the correct reading of the parable, 'oil' in the parable stands for acts of obedience. Just as in the parable of the Feast it was not satisfactory simply to be there – it was necessary to have the appropriate wedding garment, and the wedding garment stood for good works – so in the parable of the Ten Virgins it is essential for those who wait for the Bridegroom to have oil; and 'oil' stands for good works. The wise have plenty; the foolish have not. 'Watching' and being ready for the coming of the Bridegroom means using well the time given to us and using it in particular for good works. Is then the message of the parable exactly the same as the message of the Feast? Not altogether. They are similar in their emphasis on good works. Good works are part of 'being ready' for the kingdom. But in the parable of the Ten Virgins there is a conversation between the wise and the foolish which introduces a different dimension. The wise have enough oil for themselves to get their own torches going, but not enough to share with the foolish (v.8): *The foolish said to the prudent, 'Our lamps are going out; give us some of your oil.' 'No,' they answered; 'there will never be enough for all of us. You had better go to the dealers and buy some for yourselves'.* But this proves to be more easily said than done. Buying oil during the night is, they discover to their cost, more difficult than they imagined. So if the parable is about death intervening to shorten the time available for good works, and oil in the parable is symbolic of good works, then in terms of the overall message of the parable the conversation between the wise and foolish virgins raises and answers a question: Can the good works of other people help us to gain entry into the kingdom? They can inspire us and encourage us. But their good works can never take the place of our own. The answer is clearly 'No!' So the function of the young girls, which was to go out with torches in the bridegroom's procession as he goes out to meet the bride, can only be fulfilled by those who are prepared. (The REB translation 'lamps' is inadequate; the picture is of torches capable of being used in procession through the night air.) Those who are ready and prepared for the procession, enter the banquet hall and the banquet begins. The foolish finally arrive: *'Sir, sir, open the door for us,' they cried. But he answered, 'Truly I tell you: I do not know you'* (see 7.23). So the parable ends with its main concern: *Keep awake then, for you know neither the day nor the hour*, and keeping awake means acting responsibly before God.

I. The Talents

25.14–30

The next parable, the Talents, is to be found in both Matthew and Luke. Its Matthean form has several distinctive features. In Matthew's version of the Talents, when the master goes abroad he distributes to his servants to *each according to his ability* (v.15). The phrase evokes a 'harvest' passage from Deuteronomy. It includes the promise that a good farmer will benefit both from divine generosity and from his own God-given ability (see Deuteronomy 16.17). The richness of the harvest is the result of both. The parable seems to point in the same direction. The master shows considerable generosity to his servants; the ability of the servants also plays its part. The two together can produce a substantial profit. We have already noted earlier a second distinctive element in the Matthean form of parable: the response of the third servant was one of fear: *Then the man who had been given one bag came and said, 'Master, I knew you to be a hard man: you reap where you have not sown, you gather where you have not scattered; so I was afraid, and I went and hid your gold in the ground'* (vv.24f.). His reaction to his master's generosity in giving each a task and the means to complete it, inhibits him and distorts his understanding of the master's motives. The servant makes him out to be hard-hearted and grasping. The result is catastrophic. Fear turns the episode sour and the third servant is expelled empty-handed and punished as *lazy* and unprofitable. Fear is a disabler. The parable belongs with the Feast and the Ten Virgins. Like them it is about human responses to divinely given opportunities. The responses in the parables are sometimes positive, and sometimes grudging and fearful. But to what context do they belong? What are these divinely given opportunities? Are they opportunities of service within the Christian community? Or is at least one level of interpretation the practical level of the narrative itself. The parable would then be a probing of practical attitudes to the use of money. It is about day-to-day decisions and the attitudes which inform them. The kingdom of Heaven is about these. It is about finance and the handling of what is entrusted to us. And success and failure have surprising consequences, out of all proportion to the tasks described. For the one there is the joy of sharing in the master's work (vv 21f.); for the other there is pain and rejection (v.30).

J. The Sheep and the Goats
25.31–46

In the final parable of Matthew, the Sheep and the Goats, daily behaviour is judged by the Son of Man, as King and Judge of all. In a vision the far-off final moment of reckoning becomes a present reality. Sometimes the interpretation of the Sheep and the Goats has been restricted to the question of how Christians have been helped or rejected. The 'little ones' are identified as Christian missionaries arriving in some town or village. But for two reasons that should be rejected: first, Matthew's gospel has often reminded us that the little ones, the weak and the vulnerable, go before us into the kingdom. It is they, not the Christian missionaries, who have pride of place at the Last Judgement; second, the standards of judgement – feeding the hungry, giving water to the thirsty, caring for the stranger, clothing the naked, visiting the sick and caring for the imprisoned – suggest that to concentrate only on the missionaries would be far too narrow an interpretation. Furthermore all the criteria can be supported from Gentile as well as Jewish sources. All the nations are here before the judgement-seat and the judgement of all hangs on their treatment of their needy neighbours. The extraordinary feature of the vision is that neither those who had cared nor those who had not cared were aware of what they had done: '*Lord, when was it that we saw you hungry and fed you, or thirsty and gave you drink, a stranger and took you home, or naked and clothed you? When did we see you ill or in prison, and come to visit you?*' (vv.37–39). This stress on ignorance is bewildering. Surely Matthew's gospel has been concerned with good works done with a clear and obvious intention. Again and again the emphasis has been on the deliberate motive behind actions. How then can the final judgment take account only of the action itself? The answer could be that we are not being asked to take account only of the action in itself. We are being asked to see both the simplicity and the complexity of loving actions. Throughout the gospel Matthew has been interested in Jesus as the teacher who asked for a new awareness of what it means to do what is right. Here in the final Discourse the most difficult issue of all is exposed: we cannot always know when we do what is right. God's will in each particular circumstance may not be evident. Often we have to act in faith. That may not be what we expected to find in Matthew's gospel. We are accustomed to thinking of Paul as the one who commends faith, and Matthew as the one who commends law. But Matthew's gospel is not so easily summarized. The final parable asks us to face our inadequacies of understanding and awareness. We cannot always know what is God's will. And hidden within the uncertainties of daily behaviour is a further mystery. We are given the promise: To risk yourself for those in need is to meet Christ, and to meet Christ is to find God in our midst: '*Truly I tell you: anything you did for one of my brothers here, however insignificant, you did for me*' (v.40). Matthew's gospel offers this promise in various different circumstances. The presence of the living Christ is with us: He is present where two or three are gathered in his name (18.20); he is present wherever and when-ever his disciples baptize and teach (28.20); he is also present in the daily encounter with those in need. This is a promise for every day, in the middle of all our uncertainties and questions: God in Christ is with us.

> Your labour which proceeds from love,
> Jesus shall generously approve, . . .
> with brightest crowns your loan repay,
> and tell you in that joyful day,
> 'Ye did it unto me'. (*SFP* 29)

The judgement happens, and judgement is part of our everyday experience. Faith is our way to life; but the obverse is also true: the avoiding of risk is death.

§14 The Trial and the Crucifixion of Jesus
26.1–27.66

A. Prophecies and Plots
26.1–16

The Final Discourse is complete (v.1). It ends with the Son of Man in glory, judging all the nations of the world. The Passion Narrative begins with the same Son of Man arrested, unjustly condemned by a human court, and handed over to be crucified: *'You know that in two days' time it will be Passover, when the Son of Man will be handed over to be crucified'* (v.2; see Mark 14.1, where the name Son of Man does not appear). The reversal of roles is poignant and dramatic. We see the Judge of all as the one who is unjustly judged; we see the one who is crucified as one who will ultimately be vindicated. That reversal of roles is an essential feature of Matthew's good news. The handing over of the Son of Man is to occur at Passover time. The Passover was the feast which celebrated the protection of the people of Israel from the angel of death and enabled the exodus from Egypt to happen. It began with the slaughtering of the lambs on the afternoon of 14th Nisan, ready for the Passover meal at sundown and was a period for reliving the Exodus and for thanksgiving to God for his deliverance from slavery, from darkness and from distress. There was an overlap between the Passover and the feast of Unleavened Bread, so that in effect the festival period lasted from 14th to 21st Nisan. *In two days' time* might therefore be a reference to a day in the week in which the Passover happened; reckoned inclusively this would be 13th Nisan; if an inclusive reckoning is not appropriate it might mean 12th or 11th Nisan. The phrase might however refer to a moment of great significance (Exodus 19.16) rather than to a particular day of the week; the great moment of the world's deliverance is at hand. The irony of the following verse lies in the fact that, according to the gospel account, Jesus has seized the initiative in choosing to face death. The Jewish leaders thought that they were in charge; the chief priests and the elders of the people met in the house of the high priest, Caiaphas, and discussed a scheme to seize Jesus and put him to death (vv.3–4f.). The arrest of Jesus is planned by *the chief priests and the elders of the people*. They now take the centre of the stage; the Pharisees and scribes move into the background. V.5 (*'It must not be during the festival'*) recognizes that a popular uprising must be avoided at all costs. All the same the festival of Unleavened Bread arrives (26.17) and the plot has still not been carried out.

26.6f.   A feature of the good news is his anointing by a woman in Bethany (John 12.3–8 gives her the name Mary). It is a costly act (v.7), resented by the disciples as a wicked waste (v.8; see 20.11 and contrast Mark 14.4), but commended by Jesus (v.9) and regarded by him as a priority (even over the poor, v.11) and as preparing him for his death (v.12). The disciples do not understand; but a woman does. Following the commendation in the previous chapters of those who feed the poor, such an extravagance might seem incongruous. V.9 implies as much. But seen as a prophetic act, deeply personal in its generosity, it is far from incongruous. It has an inner consistency with the good news which apart from all its other rich associations celebrates the historic place of women within the Jesus story. What follows presents several contrasts between the anointing and betrayal. For the woman in Bethany nothing is too much; for Judas Jesus is worth no more than the traditional worth of a slave (Exodus 21.32). For the one the meal is an opportunity for devotion; for the other it is a time for treachery. Because of its consistency with the gospel the story of the anointing will continue to be told through the world (v.13) *as her memorial*. Again there is a sudden contrast: by contrast with the woman's affectionate action, Judas Iscariot for no explicit reason, but apparently for financial gain, asks the chief priests *'What will you give me to betray him to you?'* (v.15a). The agreement of *thirty silver pieces* (v.15b) points forward to the quotation from Zechariah 11.12, where in the Zechariah context the shepherd of the flock delivers the sheep to the false shepherds for destruction at the price of thirty shekels of silver.

B. The Last Supper
26.17–29

The Last Supper includes Jesus' prophecy that one of the twelve would betray him (v.21), and each one in turn denies responsibility (v.22). That someone actually eating with him should betray him (v.23) is given great emphasis, as is the warning that fulfilling the scriptures, as the events move toward the crucifixion, will not exonerate the traitor (v.24). To Judas' question: '*Rabbi, surely you do not mean me?*' Jesus replies: '*You have said it.*' The reader is thus fully aware that Jesus knows the traitor's identity, but will not interfere with the march of events. The Last Supper is also a prophetic act, performed by Jesus as a self-commitment to seal God's covenant with his own death, and as a means of constituting his disciples as a continuing witness to his mission. Shared with his disciples, the meal with its fourfold action (took, blessed, broke, gave) points beyond that immediate time and place in two specific respects. First it is according to Matthew *the blood of the covenant, shed for many for the forgiveness of sins* (v.28). This is an unexpected association of covenant blood and forgiveness of sins. The reference to forgiveness is not surprising. Despite the contrast between Matthew 3.4 and Mark 1.4, we have seen a number of places in Matthew where forgiveness is available for those who repent, not least in relation to meals eaten with tax-gatherers and sinners. But the specific association of forgiveness with covenant blood is unexpected, because it has no parallel elsewhere in Matthew and because forgiveness of sins does not belong within the early Passover tradition. Presumably it developed from the Marcan tradition in Mark 14.24 'This is my blood, the blood of the covenant, shed for many' in communities where specific provisions were made for the declaration of forgiveness and where that forgiveness was linked either with God's covenant or with the death of the obedient Son or with both (see Jeremiah 31.34; Matthew 1.21). The presence of the disciples is significant. Jesus' self-commitment concerns them particularly. He offers them bread and wine in the sharing of which they become his body: '*Take this and eat; this is my body*' (v.26). But it is not only for them; it is for the wider world as well. So, second, Jesus also points toward a future banquet in which all God's people will share: '*Never again shall I drink from this fruit of the vine until that day when I drink it new with you in the kingdom of my Father*' (v.29); either this prophecy is linked with his personal refusal to share in drinking from the cup (as some suggest) as an act of renouncing present protection and solace, or (more likely), it is a warning that this cup will be the last he shares with them on earth.

C. Peter's Promise
26.30–35

The REB refers to the *singing* of *the Passover hymn* (v.30) which followed the Last Supper as Jesus and his disciples left the room for the mount of Olives. It may indeed have been the case at the original Last Supper that the Passover psalmody was sung. But in Matthew's time that need not have been the case, as by then a different form of eucharistic song began to develop; so REB's addition of *Passover* in v.30 could be misleading. The story continues with another contrast. At the Last Supper the disciples are constituted as the continuing means of God's mission. Immediately their coming apostasy, together with the dispersal of all his followers, is signalled: '*Tonight you will all lose faith because of me; for it is written: "I will strike the shepherd and the sheep of his flock will be scattered"*' (v.31; see Zechariah 13.7). The text of Zechariah 13.7 in Matthew 26.31 differs from the LXX in the use of the phrase ' I will strike', in the singular 'the shepherd' (see the Damascus Document 19.7–13 for a similar use), and in the twofold form of Matthew 26.31 (see the Epistle of Barnabas 5.12). '*The sheep of his flock*' has a wide reference and does not apply only to the disciples;[1] and although there are several quotations from Zechariah in the Passion Narratives it is difficult to identify a single apologetic or theological purpose behind their use, apart of course from the general purpose of showing how scripture has been fulfilled in the story of his passion. If v.31 had a reference to a wide group of people, all of whom forsake him, v.32 '*But after I am raised, I shall go ahead of you into Galilee*' has a somewhat narrower reference (how much narrower is not clear even when the prophecy is fulfilled in 28.16–17; see §15D which considers if a group other than the eleven may have been mentioned). Peter's response is again hasty and over-confident; his vow that he will never abandon Jesus

---

[1]See H. Stegemann, *RevQ* 14, 1963, pp. 235–70, for the Qumran approach to Psalm 37 in 4Qp Ps 37, and its parallel in Matthew 5.3

or find offence in him (v.33) is met by Jesus' prophecy *'Truly I tell you: tonight before the cock crows you will disown me three times'* (v.34). The triple disowning of Jesus provides a significant pattern for the later stages of the Passion Narrative, both with respect to Peter's role and that of Jesus himself. Unaware of this, Peter repeats his vow of faithfulness, which all the disciples echo (v.35).

D. Gethsemane
26.36–46

26.36 *Jesus then came with his disciples to a place called Gethsemane.* In the garden of Gethsemane on the slopes of Mount Olivet he separates himself first from all but Peter and the two sons of Zebedee. Then, as he moves away from them, he is overwhelmed with grief (v.37; see 20.22): *Distress and anguish overwhelmed him, and he said to them, 'My heart is ready to break with grief. Stop here, and stay awake with me.'* Then he himself went on a little farther . . . and prayed (vv.38–39a). The quotation from Zechariah (v.31) declares that the coming crisis is divinely caused. For Jesus this raises the issue of obedience in its most testing form. It is this issue which underlies the Gethsemane narrative: *'My Father'* he prays, *'if it is possible, let this cup pass me by . . .'* What he does now is in his unique role as God's Son. Twice Matthew recounts his prayer of obedience, the second time using the very words which he had taught his disciples. He taught them to say 'Your will be done' (Matthew 6.10). Now in this critical moment Jesus shows what that means and how costly it is to pray that prayer: *'Yet not my will but yours'* (v.39c). The promise that whatever we ask will be honoured has already been qualified in a number of ways. Now the ultimate qualification is offered : the will of the Father. The threefold repetition of the prayer underlines its cost; and the return of Jesus to the disciples underlines their thoughtlessness and unreliability. The moment is unique, coming before his betrayal, trial and crucifixion. But it is a pattern for all his disciples to follow in every crisis of obedience to God. It is an example of what 'watching' involves. Jesus came back to the disciples and found them asleep: *and he said to Peter, 'What! Could none of you stay awake with me for one hour? Stay awake, and pray that you may be spared the test'* (again see the Lord's Prayer; 6.13). The disciples sleep; the Son of Man prays. The contrast points up the distinction between Jesus and his disciples: *'The spirit is willing, but the flesh is weak'* (v.41). The triple nature of the event in Gethsemane (v.44) matches the other threefold patterns before and after Gethsemane. The passage concludes with the dramatic announcement: *'The hour has come! The Son of Man is betrayed into the hands of sinners. Up, let us go! The traitor is upon us.'*

E. The Betrayal
26.47–56

The Gethsemane scene is interrupted by the arrival of Judas with a large crowd, *sent by the chief priests and the elders of the nation* (v.47; see Jeremiah 18.18). On the whole in these accounts Matthew's gospel follows Mark. There are slight deviations in the conversation between Jesus and Judas, and these make even more intense in Matthew the transformation of traditional acts of affection into the means of betrayal: *Going straight up to Jesus, he said, 'Hail, Rabbi!' and kissed him* (v.49). Judas thus makes it certain that it is Jesus they apprehend. The response of Jesus (v.50) is found only in Matthew and Luke, and in Matthew it has variant translations. Some translations understand the verse as a question: 'Friend, what are you here for?' Others suggest that Jesus' reply shows that he knew what Judas intended to do and that he himself could take the initiative: *'Friend, do what you are here to do!'* (REB). The latter is certainly more in keeping with the picture of Jesus in Matthew's Passion Narrative. He is in control of events throughout the story: They may seize him (v.50b). The requirement that the scriptures should be fulfilled is twice emphasized by Matthew in these verses, once on the lips of Jesus (v.54) and once as a comment by the evangelist (v.56). There is no need for the disciples to take action to defend him; the arrest must take its course. To the drawing of a sword and the cutting off of the servant's ear (v.51) Jesus responds with a comment which is unique to Matthew. It renounces physical force, and adds: *'All who take the sword die by the sword'* (v.52). He renounces the use of physical force; he also renounces the use of spiritual powers (v.53); the arrest must run its course as the prophets foretold. The same message is given to the crowd (v.55): the arrest must run its course, so there is no need for secrecy or for a show of force, and never has been. At this point the disciples desert him (v.56). The Son of Man is alone and a prisoner.

F. *Accusations and Denials*
26.57–75

26.57 *Jesus was led away under arrest to the house of Caiaphas the high priest, where the scribes and elders were assembled*. While Peter, outside in the *high priest's courtyard*, awaits the outcome (v.58; or is it 'the end'?), the trial continues within. The narrative of the trial before the Jewish officials bristles with difficulties both legal and historical, but there is no indication that Matthew had any interest in these. The interrogation takes a threefold form in which the questions are progressively sharper, and the responses progressively clearer. In the course of the investigation three areas are examined: first, general allegations which might warrant a death sentence (v.59); second, that he said '*I can pull down the temple of God, and rebuild it in three days*' (v.61), for which the evidence is inconclusive, and Jesus neither admits the charge nor denies it (vv.62f.); and, third, is he *the Messiah, the Son of God*? (v.63). The answer of Jesus in Matthew is strange. Whereas in Mark Jesus answers 'I am' (14.62), in Matthew and Luke Jesus avoids the direct answer: in Matthew '*The words are yours*' (see Luke 22.67f.) is followed by a substitute response : '*from now on you will see the Son of Man seated at the right hand of the Almighty and coming on the clouds of heaven*' (v.64). The meaning of this in the context of the whole gospel is clear: this is the moment (*from now on*) when the one who is himself unjustly condemned is vindicated, when he establishes the standards for the judgement of all humanity as the Son of Man, humiliated and vindicated. The verdict of blasphemy declared by the high priest (v.65) is imprecise, but in Matthean terms entirely intelligible. The claim implied in Jesus' answer is as unacceptable to Jewish leaders of Matthew's own day as in Jesus' day a self-reference to the Danielic Son of Man would have been.

After the verdict of blasphemy there follows the humiliation of the prisoner, the 'spitting and beating' of v.67 (see Isaiah 50.6). Four different references to prophecy occur in this section. The first, explicit in Mark but not in Matthew, concerns the destruction and rebuilding of the temple. It is strange that Mark and Matthew should differ as to whether or not this constituted false evidence. Both record prophetic words of Jesus about the destruction of the temple (Mark 13.2; Matthew 24.2), although neither provides an exact quotation of such a prophecy in the story of the trial. The second prophecy concerns the coming of the Son of Man. The third case of prophecy belongs to the mocking of Jesus (v.68): '*Now, Messiah, if you*

163

are a prophet, tell us who hit you.' Jesus was, as Mark says, blindfolded, so that the mockery was either a further test of his claims, or the means by which the chief priests were officially dissociating themselves from a blasphemer. Ironically, and Matthew would have appreciated the irony, what they achieved by mocking Christ was further evidence that in the history of Jesus the prophets were being fulfilled. Finally there is the fulfilment of Christ's own prophecy that Peter would deny him three times. Peter fails, denies his Lord, but survives and remains a disciple, becoming a major leader in the history of the early church. That he could survive as a disciple despite a threefold denial of Christ is a witness to the power of forgiveness exercised by and in the name of Christ. That is how Matthew understood the situation. The story is told without any attempt to suggest mitigating circumstances. Peter failed, as Jesus had prophesied that he would. Nowhere is the record challenged. Indeed it is very hard to imagine circumstances in which anyone could have invented such an astonishing story: the fall and restitution of a leading disciple to whom the greatest possible promises had been made. The story of Peter's entrance into the high priest's courtyard and the three subsequent denials follow the pattern of the trial before Caiaphas. The first of the three accusations comes privately from a *servant-girl* (v.69): *'You were with Jesus the Galilean'*, and Peter's denial is made publicly (v.70). The second is more public: another girl *said to the people there, 'He was with Jesus of Nazareth'* (v.71), and Peter's denial is accompanied by an oath (v.72; see §3E). The third comes from a bystander and is more threatening: *'You must be one of them; your accent give you away!'* (v.73), and Peter begins to curse and swear and he denies all knowledge of Jesus. The cock crows, and Peter remembers Jesus' prophecy (v.75). The net has closed tighter and tighter, and Peter's denial has become more and more public and vehement. It has the same pattern as the trial of Jesus, and the threefold repetition of the question would have been frighteningly reminiscent of the official interrogation of Christians in times of persecution. Peter has failed; and he weeps in bitter anguish.

G. Pilate and Judas
27.1–10

27.1 In the morning the plan to have Jesus put to death is complete, and he is handed over bound to *the Roman governor* Pontius *Pilate* (v.2). When Judas sees that Jesus has been condemned he is *seized with remorse* (v.3), and returns the thirty pieces of silver. Judas uses a significant description for Jesus; he calls him 'innocent' (see 27.19,24; Jeremiah 19.4): *'I have brought an innocent man to his death'* (v.4). So when the leaders of the people pay no attention to him' Judas throws *the money down in the temple* (see Zechariah 11.13 LXX), and goes and hangs himself (v.5). This poses for the leaders the problem of what to do with the money, since it *cannot be put into the temple fund* (v.6; some scholars ascribe this point in the narrative to a Syriac version of Zechariah 11.13). So the Jewish leaders *buy the Potter's Field, as a burial-place for foreigners* (v.7). The prophecy is thus fulfilled, a prophecy which provides a test of ingenuity for anyone. In Acts 1.18f. Judas' death is a sudden seizure in a 'Field of Blood' bought by Judas; in Matthew the name 'Field of Blood' is associated with 'blood money' and the chief priests designate the silver for the purpose of a cemetery for strangers. Those two stories are hard to reconcile. What has happened, we are told by Matthew, fulfils a prophecy. But where does the prophecy come from? The prophecy and the story recall elements from Jeremiah 18.2; 19.3–15; 32.9, Zechariah 11.13 and Lamentations 4.2 (as well as variants and versions of those texts); but the citation in vv.9f. allows no exact identification. An important parallel to this passage is the reference to the spilling of innocent blood by a tyrant in Matthew 2.17–19, where another reference to Jeremiah appears (see §1F). Violence, injustice and the shedding of blood are common elements in the story of Jeremiah and of Jesus, and 27.3–10 illustrates the similarity powerfully.

H. The Roman Governor
27.11–26

27.11 Jesus is brought before Pilate, whose first question reveals the changed character of the case which the chief priests have brought against Jesus: *'Are you the king of the Jews?'* The charge of blasphemy on which the night council had condemned him has been changed into a political charge of treason. Again the response of Jesus is ambiguous: *'The words are yours.'* V.12 narrates that charges were then brought by the high priests and elders. Their content is left undefined, but the conclusion suggests that they were corroborative of the treason charge. To Pilate's *great astonishment* Jesus makes no response (vv.13f.). Matthew is here following Mark closely (v.15): *it was customary for the governor to release one prisoner chosen by the people.* There is no evidence for this custom and this part of the narrative is suspect from a historical point of view. The release by a Roman governor of a notorious trouble-maker like Barabbas (v.16) is highly unlikely (see however the omission in v.16 of the major part of Mark's description of Barabbas). Matthew makes a significant change to Pilate's question to the Jewish people: instead of using the charge 'King of the Jews' Pilate refers to him as *Jesus called Messiah* (v.17), and the REB matches Jesus the Messiah with an ancient reading *'Jesus Barabbas'.* Like Mark Matthew attributes the charge against Jesus to *malice* (literally 'envy') and makes clear that this motivation had not escaped Pilate.

27.19   *While Pilate was sitting in court a message came to him from his wife.* Once again we have a link with the Birth Narratives (see §1C). His wife has had a disturbing dream, and she warns Pilate to *have nothing to do with that innocent man.* (The themes of Jesus' innocence and of Gentile understanding receive further support.) Evidence that the dream material has been inserted into the narrative comes from the following verses. The beginning of v.20, *Meanwhile,* suggests that the episode of the message also covers the time during which the high priests and elders could be active among the crowd. But when the governor puts his question in v.21 it is apparent that this is the question put in v.17 when the people assembled, and not (as in Mark 15.12) an additional question. The flow of the Marcan narrative has been lost. No part of Matthew's gospel is quite so open to the charge of anti-Semitism as that which now follows. The crowd chooses Barabbas and demands that Jesus called Messiah be crucified (v.22), a demand that grows as Pilate asks what harm Jesus has done. As Pilate washes his hands in full view of the crowd (v.24), and passes the responsibility over to them (*'See to that yourselves'*) the crowd appears to involve the whole Jewish community in the condemnation of Jesus: *'His blood be on us and on our children'* (v.25). But how did Matthew intend this passage to be heard? Probably it was not intended as a self-curse nor as a signing of a nation's eternal fate. In Matthew's account it need not be either of these. The narrative suggests no more than that a particular community accepted a responsibility of which Pilate tried to wash his hands. Granted it was a responsibility for themselves and the following generation, but there is nothing to suggest that Matthew heard this or intended this as the acceptance of a curse on the people for all time. So Jesus is handed over, to be crucified (v.26).

I. The Mocking of Jesus
27.27–31

What in Luke's gospel happens in Herod Antipas' residence happens in Matthew in *the Praetorium* (v.27), the governor's residence, and after Pilate's judgement, not before it as in John's gospel. Jesus is decked out as a king with royal robe, sceptre and crown, for further mockery and abuse (v.28). The mockery brings together in a single scene the injustice of how Jesus was treated and the reality of his kingship: *Falling on their knees before him they jeered at him: 'Hail, king of the Jews!'* (v.29; see 2.2) It is difficult to provide a consecutive account of the trial which harmonizes the details from all of the gospels. On the other hand archaeological finds in Jerusalem give some support to the Johannine and Matthean narrative here. Rather than possessing a consecutive narrative we have a series of deftly portrayed scenes, like the conscripting of Simon of Cyrene to carry Jesus' cross (v.32). The purpose of the scenes is to build up the contrast with which the Passion Narrative began, between the innocent Son of God, judged unjustly by his own people, and the one who enters his kingdom.

J. The Crucifixion
27.32–66

Matthew is still following the Marcan outline. The conscripting of Simon of Cyrene to carry the cross (v.32), the offering of wine to Jesus (in Matthew mixed with gall; v.34) to dull the pain, the quotation of Psalm 22.18 regarding the casting of lots for his clothes (v.35), and the setting of the titulus over his head with the charge

'*The king of the Jews*' inscribed upon it (v.37), are all part of the Marcan narrative. They intensify the event of the crucifixion itself; the one who suffers is the one who reigns. In Matthew's narrative of the crucifixion there is a clear focus on the sonship of Jesus. At three places in the story of the crucifixion reference is made to the 'Son of God', and the first two of these appear only in Matthew. The third has a context unique to Matthew. The first (v.40) recalls the temptations, '. . . if you are God's Son' (4.3, 6): *So you are the man who was to pull down the temple and rebuild it in three days! If you really are the Son of God, save yourself and come down from the cross.*' The context is similar to that of the second temptation: 'Save yourself and come down from the cross.' But sonship involves obedience. It has, as in Gethsemane, its bitter side, symbolized in the drink given to Jesus in v.34, 'wine mixed with gall'. As in Gethsemane there is no way for the Son of God except that of obedience, to the bitter end. The second reference is added to a quotation which closely resembles Psalm 22.8. '*He trusted in God, did he? Let God rescue him – for he said he was God's Son*' (v.43). It is one of several links between Matthew 27.33–54 and Psalm 22. Those who *wagged their heads and jeered at him* (v.39) provide an echo of Psalm 22.7, and Psalm 22.8 reads 'Let the Lord deliver him, for he holds him dear!' There is of course no reference to 'Son of God' in Psalm 22. For that we have to turn to the Matthean temptations, or in the Old Testament to passages such as the Wisdom of Solomon 2.18. One who is God's Son can expect God to save him (see 27.43); the sufferer will be delivered. But there is no way for Jesus to avoid death. The darkness everywhere is a portent of dreadful events of judgement (v.45) and there is a cry from the cross '*Eli, Eli*' . . . '*My God, my God*' (v.46). It quotes the opening of Psalm 22 and carries with it an expectation of divine presence even in the darkness of death: '*Why have you forsaken me?*' Some bystanders understand Eli as a call to Elijah (the form of the quotation in Matthew can be understood in that sense, and Elijah was expected to come the help of the upright in danger: v.47). One of the bystanders offers sour wine on a sponge (v.48; see Psalm 69.21), while others understand the call to Elijah as a useless appeal to a dead prophet (17.12), or a further opportunity for mockery (v.49: *Let us see if Elijah will come to save him*). The humiliation of God's Son is complete; all the ways of deliverance are closed to him.

The third and final reference to 'Son of God' follows the death of Jesus: *Jesus again cried aloud and breathed his last* (v.50). There is the splitting of the temple veil (v.51), the earthquake, the opening of the graves and the rising of the saints (v.52) who enter the city after the resurrection (v.53). Although the detail of these events does not harmonize easily with the later Matthean resurrection narrative, the impact of these events is obvious: This is the death of the Son of God and it is a cosmic happening. All that occurs marks it as a momentous event. So when the Roman centurion gives his testimony to Jesus as Son of God in v.54 (*'This must have been a son of God'*), it is not because of the noble character of his death; it is because of its shattering effect. This is the Son of God of the 'walking on the water'. There, and at his death and at his rising from the dead, the signs of divine activity are there for all to see.

27.55 *A number of women were also present, watching from a distance.* Although women have only occasionally occupied a central place in the Matthean story of Jesus, they have an important role. Here, immediately after the death of Christ, the first of his followers to be mentioned are women. During his lifetime they had *looked after him* and Zebedee's wife, who brought her sons to Jesus asking for a special place for them and who had been told that their cup would be a cup of suffering, is a witness with the two Maries to the full cost of following Jesus. The two Maries, Mary of Magdala and Mary the mother of James and Joseph, also have a part to play. Joseph of Arimathaea, who in Matthew is given the designation 'discipled to Jesus' (v.57), had asked Pilate for the body of Jesus and with Pilate's permission, *wrapped it in a clean linen sheet, and laid it in his own unused tomb*. The events of the first day of the week are hinted at in v.60. *He then rolled a large stone against the entrance* . . . It is there, by the tomb, that the women sit. In this way the narrator has prepared the reader for two subsequent events. The speed with which Joseph had the body of Jesus released for burial might, in Matthew's narrative, have given rise to questions about his motives: Had he planned that the body should be stolen, or attempts be made to revive it? So there will be the story of how the chief priests and the Pharisees secured the tomb against theft. And, more important for the resurrection narratives, the women know where to go in order to visit the tomb.

Matthew's version of the burial of Jesus logically leads to the final narrative of the Passion story, the narrative of the securing of the tomb. But where did the story come from? Almost certainly in the form in which we have it the story is a fiction. The Pharisees appear here for the first time in the Passion Narrative (v.62); the *next day* was a sabbath and no Jew would have organized a deputation on a sabbath morning; in any case the next morning would be like locking the stable door after the horse had bolted; and if the disciples had temporarily forgotten the promise of resurrection, how likely is it that their enemies would have remembered it: *'we recall how that impostor said while he was still alive "I am to be raised again after three days"'* (v.63). It must surely have been a fiction, composed to answer the charge that disciples had stolen the corpse (*'Otherwise his disciples may come and steal the body, and then tell the people that he has been raised from the dead'*). It was not Matthew's story; it did not answer the charge that they had revived the corpse. In Mark Pilate checked that Jesus was already dead; not so in Matthew (see v.66), where Pilate simply gives permission and has the tomb sealed (vv.65f.). From the point of view of the general reader Mark's narrative was the stronger. But it seems that for Matthew that did not matter. What mattered for Matthew was not charge and counter-charge, but that Jesus was risen, a living Lord among his people.

§15 His Resurrection and Universal Authority
28.1–20

A. At Daybreak
28.1–7

In Matthew's gospel the resurrection narrative begins as dawn breaks: *About daybreak on the first day of the week* (v.1). That is probably the best way to interpret the somewhat confusing time reference. It begins with the same account which Mark has. It records the coming of the two women to the Jerusalem tomb. They knew where the tomb was and they went to see it. The Marcan details about what the women intended to do are missing. There is no mention of buying in spices, of preparing them as in Luke, or of intending to anoint the corpse. Matthew's account suggests a return to the graveside. They are returning to grieve. At that point the story takes a decisively new turn. In Mark the women are concerned about the size of the stone at the mouth of the tomb. How are they to roll it aside? If they are to anoint the body they must have help, and help may not be available. In Matthew there are no such worries. There is a violent earthquake and a miraculous removal of the stone that seals the tomb (v.2); there is a supernatural vision of the shining angel who has removed the stone (v.3); and the guards lie prostrate, paralysed with fear (v.4). Just as in the narrative of the crucifixion, the cosmic significance of Christ's death is conveyed in the lurid colours of earthquake and opening graves, so the heightened description of the resurrection morning awakens a sense of elation and wonder at what has happened. The language of light and brilliance stirs the emotions and provides a sense of victory. As the angelic figure is described, the power implied in the claim that Christ is risen is given symbolic expression (v.6). The message given by the angelic figure is that there is no need to fear. The prophecies by Jesus of his own rising have been fulfilled. Furthermore, the message that he is risen is to be given to his disciples. He will await them in Galilee, and will see them there (v.7). In Matthew that meeting will signal the beginning of a long history of mission and the new responsibilities of teaching and baptizing. The story which began with angelic messengers quelling the fears of Joseph and making preparation for Emmanuel, 'God with us', ends with angelic messengers quelling the fears of the women and making preparations for work in the presence of Emmanuel, to the end of time.

B. Jesus Meets the Women
28.8–10

In Mark, according to the normal ending of that gospel, the women fail to carry out their commission. Apparently from fear and terror they remain silent. In the shorter ending of Mark (the one which ends at Mark 16.8) we do not hear how the disciples received the message about Jesus meeting them in Galilee. In Matthew elation and wonder have taken the place of fear. The angelic messenger has soothed their fears; the associations of the angelic presence are joy and wonder: *They hurried away from the tomb in awe and great joy* (v.8). With no inhibitions the women give the disciples a full report, as in Luke's gospel. What follows in Matthew is a similar kind of narrative. It closely resembles the angelic vision; it is an 'appearance' narrative. But what is different is that it is Jesus who meets them. This is what distinguishes it from an angelic vision. The women are not expecting him; he greets them, says to them '*Do not be afraid*' and gives them a commission: '*Go and take word to my brothers that they are to leave for Galilee. They will see me there*' (v.10). The appearance of Jesus adds to the narrative something quite new. There is the devotion of the women who kneel before Jesus, and there are the personal relationships emphasized particularly through the phrase in v.10 'Tell my brothers.' It is not simply the story of an 'appearance', it is a recognition narrative. The one who appears is recognized as the one whom they have known before. The context of the 'recognition' story gives this feature even more significance. It is a story which calls 'brothers' disciples who have fled at his arrest (26.56). It suggests no conditions for that relationship except that which Jesus himself has established: He had been with them. So the reference to them as 'brothers' re-establishes their identity without any hint of rebuke. Jesus repeats what the angel said about the meeting in Galilee. But it is much more than a repetition. It is a confirmation that their relationship and their hopes are now to be renewed. The promises made are in process of being fulfilled. It is not merely a confirmation of the single commission, '*They are to leave for Galilee.*' It is an opening of the door for the confirmation of the lifetime commission given to them when he first called them to be disciples.

C. *The Bribing of the Guards*
28.11–15

The gospel has almost reached its final climax. Jesus has appeared to the women alive from the dead and is about to give the disciples their great commission and the promise of his continued presence. Between those two comes a story of bribery in high places. The guards at the tomb have to be bribed (v.12) to ensure their silence over what has happened. The irony of the situation is apparent. The chief priests had feared a plot by the disciples to subvert the truth by stealing the body of Jesus and claiming that Jesus had risen. Now, caught in their own machinations, they are having to suppress the truth by bribing the guard to claim that such a plot had succeeded. They also have to offer protection for the guards in case the matter should come to the governor's ears (v.14). The episode ends with the information that the guards' story is still current in Jewish circles. These strange interludes have a dramatic function. Like interludes in classical drama they mark the passage of time. They enable the hearer to place events in a sequence and imagine the movement of characters and changes of scene. The earlier discussion of the chief priests with Pilate, unlikely though it may have been historically, marked the dramatic passage of time from the Friday of the cruci-fixion toward the second of the three days of the resurrection prophecy. Now in this final section, the bribing of the guards affords the dramatic space for the news to reach the disciples and the disciples to set off for Galilee. There is more here than dramatic interest however. The gospel writer allows us a fleeting image of contemporary life. A rumour was circulating among Jews of the day that the disciples were guilty of a hoax. They had stolen the body of Jesus and claimed that he had risen. We know that the rumour was still in circulation well over a century after Matthew's time, and so there is no difficulty in believing the gospel writer's comment. The Matthean story of the hiring and the bribing of the guard provides a witty response to such a rumour. Even if it was no more convincing as evidence against a hoax than the original rumour itself, it served its purpose not only dramatically, nor only as a reminder of how those in high places wheel and deal. It allowed the witness of the early church to be heard unencumbered by rumour: the appearances which took place after the first Easter were recorded as events of recognition. They met Jesus again.

D. The Great Commission
28.16–20

28.16   *The eleven disciples made their way to Galilee, to the mountain where Jesus had told them to meet him.* The climax to the gospel directs the reader back to the story itself. The disciples are given a world-wide commission by the Lord of all. Part of that commission is to teach what Jesus taught. The story is not outdated by its finale; rather the finale makes clear the story's continuing significance. What Jesus taught must continue to be the content of the proclamation to the end of time. The tradition must be memorized and rehearsed. Not that the disciples are any different having reached the finale. Whether they are different after the commission is a matter of conjecture. As they rejoin their Lord the text gives the impression that they remain the kind of muddled community which we have become acquainted with throughout the whole of the story: *When they saw him they knelt in worship, though some were doubtful* (v.17). In fact the text of v.17 bequeaths a final mystery to the reader. Was it just a few of the eleven who were in a state of doubt, or were they all moved by worship and doubt, or were the doubtful a separate group altogether? Translations opt for one or the other of these alternatives. The original text hardly makes crystal clear which is intended. The book ends as mysteriously as it began. Jesus approaches and claims *full authority in heaven and on earth* (v.18); what has been presented in the form of a vision before (25.31–46) is now stated as a contemporary reality. The commission of the present Lord is: *'Go to all nations and make them my disciples'* (v.19).

The task of making disciples includes two particular responsibilities. One is, as we have seen, teaching what Jesus taught. The other, given pride of place, is that of baptizing in the name of Father, Son and Holy Spirit. Baptism in the threefold name is only known in the early church in oriental, especially Syrian, sources. In comparison with the baptismal formulae in the Acts of the Apostles the use of threefold name illustrates what we have discovered throughout Matthew's gospel, an emphasis on the creative power and love of the Father in heaven, the transcendent dimensions of Spirit and the humility and suffering of the obedient Son. The suitability of the threefold name at the end of Matthew is clear. The concluding promise confirms the continuity of the story of Jesus with the story of the church. His divine presence ensures that continuity: so does the learning and rehearsing of what he taught. Since what he taught, according to Matthew's gospel, was a perpetual challenge always to be seeking God's will afresh, studying Matthew's gospel remains a disturbing and illuminating task: In that sense also it is true: *'I will be with you always, to the end of time.'*